To Beth,
The best student
That I know.

INSIGHTS, INSULTS AND INSANITY
The Best of Gary W. Tooze's Quotations of the Day!

Gary W. Tooze

This is one of the books that OBC distributes. Had a quick browse through it and found some funny and thought-provoking quotes. Hope you enjoy it.

Love Tim

SOUTHDOWNE
~ PRESS ~

ORDERS

This book is distributed by UBC Press and should be ordered from them.

Toll free fax for orders: 1-800-668-0821

e-mail: orders@ubcpress.ubc.ca

World Wide Web site: http://www.ubcpress.ubc.ca

Tooze, Gary W., 1962-
  Insights, insults and insanity

ISBN 1-894029-02-X (bound)

1. Quotations, English. I. Title.

PN6081.T66 1997   081   C97-910825-X

I laughed until I screamed.

Edvard Munch

For this, I invented the printing press?

Johann Gutenberg

After I spilled the Kkrazzy Glue on it, I just couldn't put it down.

Thomas Edison

I like to read if before I go to work.

Attila the Hun

Well executed. (Tooze, not the book.)

Joseph Stalin

It certainly cured my insomnia.

Florence Nightingale

Lie back, Mr. Tooze, and tell me again: Why do you feel this way about humanity?

Sigmund Freud

Insights, Insults and Insanity is both good and original. (Unfortunately, the large part that is good is not original, and the small part that is original is not good.)

Samuel Johnson

So who's Gary Tooze? Gary is a bachelor who lives in Toronto, Canada. Since his email service is free, he has to earn his living as the President of Internet Marketing. This company develops and promotes Internet Home Pages and Web Sites. If you're interested in this service, his web site is at http://webcom.net/~real/Gary_Tooze/resume.html. Gary also is an avid squash player and gourmet (he thinks) cook. So when he's not reading his email, he's either running around the squash court or indulging in his secret passion of cooking (and devouring) international cuisine. His favorite quotations are listed below:

There is a lot of cactus in the world, but that doesn't mean you have to sit on it.

Anon

He promised me earrings, but he only pierced my ears.

Arabian saying

If the nose of Cleopatra had been a little shorter, the whole face of the world would have been changed.

Pascal

If there is one thing I wouldn't want to be twice -ZOMBIES is both of them!

Ed Wood film

the most wasted of all days is the one without laughter.

ee cummings

The key to whatever success I have today is: Don't ask. Do.

Vikki Carr

Some people drink from the fountain of life while others just rinse and spit.

Anon

Nothing is worth more than this day.

Goethe

The man who doesn't read books has no advantage over the man that can't read them.

Mark Twain

Many a man in love with a dimple makes the mistake of marrying the whole girl.

Stephen Leacock

Editor's Note

Editor's Note is a great horse, but if you want to learn how to win at the races, read Charles Carroll's *Handicapping Speed* or Ainslie's *Complete Guide to Thoroughbred Racing*. Signing up with @Derby would also be a smart move. No, this book is not about handicapping, but it is another antidote to boredom; part of the ongoing rebellion against sanity, and it's filled with wisdom, wit and plain old ribald humor.

With the advent of the Internet came instant global written communication. Very few people have exploited its opportunities with the enthusiasm of Gary W. Tooze. Imagine sending email to virtually every country on earth, several times each week and, in return, receiving everything any of your 3250 recipients find inspiring, amusing, bizarre or just plain idiotic. Visualize sorting through this mass of electronic correspondence, selecting the best and redirecting it to your worldwide audience. This is Gary W. Tooze's *The Quotations of the Day!*, considered by many to be one of the best services available in cyberspace. This book contains the distilled wit and wisdom of the first two years of this global email experiment, the best of *The Quotations of the Day!*

In preparing this book, Gary and I faced several problems. The first involved the difficulty of selecting what to include from the abundance of material available from two years of *The Quotations of the Day!* This book is dedicated to all who have contributed to this email extravaganza, especially Inga, MaeWestern, Kirstin L., Leone R., Catherine B., Madiganb, Sharon L., Carolynn c, Kmmlau, Debbie H., Yvonne S., "Ockham's Razor", Meegs, Dale R. N., most of all his loving girlfriend Teresa, who tolerates him, and Gary's squash friends at the Academy (plus a few hundred more) who take the time to forward or write their contributions to the Q. o. t. D. You ARE *The Quotations of the Day!*

A second problem was the bland hand of political correctness. Virtually every joke insults somebody, or something. We admit there is humor in this book that picks on people because of their age, gender, profession, weight, height, and nationality, to name a few distinguishing characteristics. All we can say in our defense is that we are equal opportunity insulters. Come to think of it, there does seem to be an unfair excess of lawyer jokes in the book. But, who are we to argue with world opinion? If you can't insult a lawyer, who can you insult?

This brings up the issue of copyright. Gary W. Tooze is the author of some of these items, but by no means all. Much of the material has been submitted from around the globe and, for some of it, there is no way of establishing original authorship. As a result, it was decided to rewrite all such material and, in the process, also change names, dates, and locations. In this way, we feel nobody's copyright could have been infringed.

One final point. If, after reading this book, you can't wait for a companion volume to come out, join the international conspiracy against boredom and sign up to receive *The Quotations of the Day!* Just email Gary at garytoze@idirect.com and ask him to include you as a recipient of the list. It's a free service. While you are at it, why not visit the Web Site of our other international onslaught against sanity, where you can read a history of the 21st century and become a citizen of DeltaGlobe, a virtual reality debating society. *The Ozymandias Principles* can be found at http://webcom.net/~real/ozy/ozy.html. In closing, I should like to thank Daniel Luttmann for typing the manuscript, Diane Macdonald for typesetting it, and Ken Josephson for his excellent cover design. Sarah Foster, my wife, is to be congratulated for her proofreading, although any errors are my responsibility.

Harold D. Foster
Editor.

INSIGHTS, INSULTS AND INSANITY
The Best of Gary W. Tooze's Quotations of the Day!

To Norman Earnest William Tooze

GARY TOOZE'S
Quotations of the Day!

THE SECRET OF LIFE

Here are two rules that you must follow to ensure success in life:

1. Don't tell anybody everything you know.

2. If you were expecting more, reread 1.

HINTS ABOUT THE SECOND RULE

A gossip talks to others about you; a bore talks to you about themselves; a brilliant conversationalist talks to you about yourself.

after Lisa Kirk

The next best thing to saying a good thing yourself is to quote one.

Ralph Waldo Emerson

The cheese in a mousetrap is always free.

Anon

It's easier to fight for one's principles than to live up to them.

Alfred Adler

PSYCHIATRIC HOTLINE

If you're an obsessive-compulsive, press 1 repeatedly.

If you're co-dependant, please ask someone to press 2 for you.

If you're suffering from multiple personality disorder, press 3, 4, 5, 6, and 7.

If you're paranoid-delusional, this call is being traced. We know who you are and why you're calling us. Stay on this line.

If you're schizophrenic, a little voice will tell you which numbers to press.

If you're a manic-depressive, no matter how many numbers you press, nobody is going to answer.

2 • *Gary Tooze*

BOOKS TO READ WHEN YOU HAVE A MINUTE OR TWO

1. The Amish Telephone Directory.
2. The Kosher Pork Cookbook.
3. Mike Tyson's Guide to Dating Etiquette.
4. The Best Motivational Speeches of Dr. Kevorkian.
5. Cooking the Spotted Owl (EPA).
6. The Lebanese Guide to Sustainable Communities.
7. The Best of the Mormon Divorce Lawyers.
8. Catholic Guide to Contraception.
9. Master UNIX in Five Minutes.
10. Bob Dole: My Wild Secrets.

BUMPER STICKERS OF THE U.S.S. ENTERPRISE

1. Have you tickled a Ferengi today?
2. If you've slept with Riker, HONK!
3. Our other starship separates into FOUR!
4. One of our photon torpedoes can ruin your entire day.
5. Zero to warp 9.8 in 4 seconds!

INSIGHTS AND INSULTS

Sooner or later you've got to shoot the engineer (lawyer), or nothing will ever get done.

Anon

The brain is a wonderful organ.
It begins to work the instant you wake up and keeps going until you reach the office.

after Robert Frost

A man of words but not of deeds
Is like a garden full of weeds.

Anon

THOUGHTS FOR TODAY

Everybody soon or late, sits down to a banquet of consequences.

Robert Louis Stevenson

You must be the change you wish to see in the world.

Mahatma Gandhi

To love a thing means wanting it to live.

Confucius

Don't go around saying the world owes you a living. The world owes you nothing. It was here first.

Mark Twain

Shun idleness. It is a rust that attaches itself to the most brilliant of metals.

Voltaire

Why not upset the apple cart? If you don't, those apples are going to rot, anyway.

Anon

The believer is happy; the doubter is wise.

Hungarian proverb

There's no such thing as a tough child—if you parboil them for seven hours, they always come out tender.

W.C. Fields

DO YOU BELIEVE THIS?

The world is a comedy to those who think, a tragedy to those who feel.

Horace Walpole

It's easier to replace a dead man than a good picture.

George Bernard Shaw

Whether they give or refuse, women are glad to have been asked.

Ovid

ON TIME

Punctuality is the virtue of the bored.

Evelyn Waugh

SOBER THOUGHTS FOR TODAY

One more drink and I'd be under the host.
>   *Dorothy Parker*

Work is the curse of the drinking classes.
>   *Oscar Wilde*

Reality is an illusion that occurs due to lack of alcohol.
>   *W.C. Fields*

ON DOGS AND MEN

Dogs don't brag about their sexual conquests.

Dogs don't need to find themselves.

You're never jealous about your dog's dreams.

Gorgeous dogs don't know it.

Fleas are the worst problem you can
get from a dog
(Okay, I lied, but there is a
vaccine for rabies and you
can have the one that gave it to
you put down).

Dogs have no objection to public
displays of affection.

Dogs miss you.

Dogs love togetherness and
won't want to watch football.

Dogs are not bothered by your
intelligence.

You can teach a dog what "no"
means.

Middle-aged dogs won't leave you for a younger owner.

Dogs let you drive without stepping on the imaginary brake.

Dogs don't go bald.

TEN STEPS TO MATURITY

1. Don't criticize.
2. Act more.
3. Less repetition, more insight.
4. Greater respect, love, and reverence.
5. Treat everything and everyone with sensitivity.
6. Take responsibility for your own health.
7. Listen, don't talk.
8. Observe your own thoughts.
9. Take responsibility.
10. Cultivate discretion, the truth can hurt.

WEAK JOKE

Saint Peter found three souls outside the Pearly Gates, petitioning to enter Heaven. The first soul pleaded, "Saint Peter, I was a minister on Earth; a devout man of the cloth. My life was devoted to selflessly looking after the spiritual well-being of my flock. Can I enter Heaven?"

Saint Peter replied, "Join that queue, we'll let you know."

The second soul then explained that she'd been a physician who kept her Hippocratic Oath and had devoted her life to healing the sick, regardless of their ability to pay.

Saint Peter answered, "Join the Minister's queue, we'll let you know."

The third soul then approached Saint Peter.

"On Earth," he said, "I was the President and Chief Executive Officer of one of Europe's largest companies and I...."

Saint Peter stopped him in mid-sentence.

"Come in, come in. We're delighted to have you, but remember, in three days, you're OUT!"

CAN THIS BE TRUE?

Ignorance of certain subjects is a great part of wisdom.

Grotius

'DON'T TELL THIS TO YOUR LAWYER' JOKE

A sharp lawyer buys a $70,000 automobile and for weeks bores everyone to death with stories about his wonderful car. One day, on his way to work, a drunk in a big truck broadsides him and his car is a write-off. He crawls out of the wreckage and cries at the other driver, "How could you do that to a $70,000 customized automobile?"

The police arrive and start to question witnesses, but all the lawyer can do is moan about his $70,000 car. Finally, the policeman has had enough and says, "You lawyers are so materialistic. Look at you, your right arm has been torn off, yet all you care about is your $70,000 car." For the first time, the lawyer realizes he's lost an arm, looks down and shouts, "Good God, where's my watch?!"

YOUR COMPUTER IS UNDER ATTACK: SCAN IMMEDIATELY FOR THE FOLLOWING

BOBBITT VIRUS: Removes a very vital part of the system, which will never work as well again, even if reattached.

STAR TREK VIRUS: Goes where no virus has gone before.

HEALTH CARE VIRUS: Carries out hundreds of unnecessary tests, finds everything in perfect order and bills you for $5,500.

ARNOLD SCHWARZENEGGER VIRUS: Terminates . . . beware! It'll be back.

OPRAH WINFREY VIRUS: Your hard drive will slowly expand to 220MB. Don't be fooled, it will eventually shrink back to 70 MB and stay there.

GALLUP VIRUS: Forty percent of PC's that are infected with this lose 27 percent of their data at least 12 percent of the time (within a margin of error of 4.7 percent).

AIRLINE VIRUS: You're in New York but your data is in Tokyo, or maybe Singapore.

BUREAUCRAT VIRUS: Everything seems to be working but nothing is actually being produced.

OLLIE NORTH VIRUS: Your printer will only shred paper.

ROSS PEROT VIRUS: All components in the system are activated, just before everything quits.

JIMMY HOFFA VIRUS: Has never been found.

DID YOU KNOW THAT?

$111,111,111 \times 111,111,111 = 12,345,678,987,654,321$

Look at that statue carefully. If the horse has both of its front legs in the air, its rider died in battle; if only one is raised, the person in the saddle died of wounds received in battle; if all the horses legs are firmly on the ground, its rider died naturally.

"Samba" means to rub one's navels together.

Israeli postage stamps use only glue that is certified kosher.

It was the practice of some clans to get rid of unwelcome members by burning down their homes—hence the phrase "to be fired."

More people die each year from injuries inflicted by donkeys than are killed in aircraft accidents.

DID SHE MEAN IT?

I still miss my ex-husband, but my aim
is improving.

THE LAST WORD: EPITAPHS

On True Love
Here lies my wife.
Here let her lie!
Now she's at rest
And so am I.

Again
Here lies my poor wife,
Without bed or blankit,
But dead as a door-nail,
God be thankit.

And Again
Here lie the bones of Elizabeth
Charlotte
Born a virgin, died a harlot
She was aye a virgin at seventeen
A remarkable thing in Aberdeen.

QUESTION

What's another word for Thesaurus?

A NAUGHTY JOKE

On her front porch, a very old lady was rocking away what little time she had left. Suddenly, her fairy godmother appeared and told her that, because of the good life she had led, she had been granted three wishes.

"In that case," said the old lady, "I want to be a young princess."

Immediately, POOF!, she is a beautiful young woman.

"And your second wish?" said the fairy godmother.

The young woman thought for a moment and said, "I should like to be very, very rich."

Immediately, POOF!, the rocking chair became solid gold.

"What is your third wish?" asked the fairy godmother.

Just at that moment, the cat wanders across the porch. The young beauty turns to her godmother and asks, "Can you turn him into a handsome prince, who is madly in love with me?"

POOF! and there stands a magnificent example of manhood, dressed in finery. The young princess is shaken with passion. With a smile, the prince crosses the porch, takes her into his arms and whispers into her ear, "Bet you're sorry you had me neutered."

UNDERSTANDING MEN

For three years I dated this girl, and then she started nagging at me:
"Tell me your name. Tell me your name."

after Mike Binder

THE CRIMINAL CLASSES

The Swiss news agency reported in October that a man they had arrested for robbing a bank in Geneva claimed he was innocent. He had a concrete alibi, he'd been holding up a jewelry store at the time. Police then re-arrested him for robbing the store and began looking elsewhere for the bank bandit.

SIMPLE QUIZ FOR SIMPLETONS

Questions

1. The Canary Islands are named after what?
2. What was the first name of King George VI?
3. What is the color of the purple Finch?
4. Which country grows Chinese gooseberries?
5. In what month do the Russians celebrate the October Revolution?
6. Where do they manufacture Panama hats?
7. Catgut comes from which animal?
8. What was the length of the Hundred Years War?
9. What is used to make camel's hair brushes?
10. The Thirty Years War lasted how long?

Answers

1. Dogs—the Latin name was Insularia Canaria—Island of the Dogs.
2. Albert. Queen Victoria had requested no future king be called Albert.
3. Crimson.
4. New Zealand.
5. November.
6. Ecuador.
7. Catgut comes from sheep and horses.
8. It lasted from 1337 to 1453, 116 years.
9. Fir from squirrels.
10. Thirty years; from 1618 to 1648.

DO YOU BELIEVE THIS?

Madness takes it's toll. Please have exact change ready.

Behind an able man there are always other able men
(and usually an amazed woman).

mutilated Chinese proverb

A man is what he thinks about all day long.

Ralph Waldo Emerson

QUOTES TO REMEMBER

Once you have flown, you will walk the Earth with your eyes turned skyward,
for there you have been, there you long to return.

Da Vinci

Reality is the best metaphor.

Anon

Our doubts are traitors, and make us lose the good we oft might win,
by fearing to attempt.

William Shakespeare

I'm opposed to millionaires, but it would be dangerous to offer me the position.

Mark Twain

Everything is funny as long as it is happening to someone else!

Will Rogers

MODERN POETRY: A CRITIQUE

Last Friday I had to pick up my daughter from school to take her to the
physician. One sad child sat alone, in a corner, apparently trying to write poetry.
I glanced at her work:

> *Yesterday, yesterday, yesterday*
>
> *Contentment, contentment, contentment*
>
> *Today, today, today*
>
> *Vexation, vexation, vexation*
>
> *Tomorrow, tomorrow, tomorrow*
>
> *Regret, regret, regret.*

Very emotionally moved by this insight, I asked her the source of her inspiration.
She looked at a loss for a moment, then explained it wasn't poetry but spelling
error corrections.

I GUESS THAT'S WHY

Winston Churchill was born in a ladies' room while his mother was at a dance.

Eat one live toad for breakfast and console yourself with the thought that nothing
that bad will happen again during the rest of the day.

ON DOGS AND MEN, AGAIN

Both want more than their fair share of the bed.

Both have a strange fear of vacuum cleaners.

Both like to dominate.

Both don't ask directions.

Both tend to smell riper with age.

Neither will tell you what's bothering them.

Both mark their territory in the same way.

Both forget anniversaries.

Neither washes dishes.

Both are suspicious about the mailman.

Neither like cats.

Both pay inordinate attention to women's crotches.

ONE-LINERS (OR TWO)

We are born hungry, wet and naked. Then we have our backsides slapped.

Give me ambiguity or something else.

Lottery: a tax on idiots.

Insanity isn't a problem. I enjoy it.

More chlorine is needed for the human gene pool.

Women won't admit their age, men won't act theirs.

All generalizations are false, except this one.

Change is not inevitable, especially from a vending machine.

Puritanism: The fear that someone, someplace far away may still be happy.

Where there's a will, put my name in it.

"Criminal lawyer," aren't they all?

Hardwork may pay off in the future. Laziness pays now.

Artificial intelligence is better than authentic stupidity.

I'm bi-sexual, especially if the price is right.

WELL I SUPPOSE SO

Start a movement, eat a prune.

Anon (who would own up to that?)

All philosophy in two words-sustain and abstain.

Epictetus

The old believe everything; the middle-aged suspect everything;
the young know everything.

Oscar Wilde

If you took 5 apples from 7 apples, what would you have? . . . 5 apples.

Anon

The trouble with refusing to take your Prozac is that your colleagues will
think you're overconfident.

Anon

The Bible tells us to love our neighbours, and also to love our enemies;
probably because they are generally the same people.

G.K. Chesterton

Never mistake knowledge for wisdom.
One is for making a living. The other for making a life.

after Arthur Guiterman

The Devil's boots don't creak.

Scottish proverb

Humor is something that thrives between a person's aspirations and his
limitations. There is more logic in humor than in anything else.
Because, you see, humor is truth.

Victor Borge

Should crematoriums give discounts for burn victims?

Anon (again!)

The wind and the waves are always on the side of the ablest navigators.

Edward Gibbon

He who asks is a fool for five minutes, but he who does not remains a fool forever.

Chinese proverb

Don't allow the things you cannot do interfere with those you can.

after John Wooden

HOW TO ENDEAR YOURSELF TO OTHERS

1. Leave the copier set to reduce 170%, very dark, 17 inch paper, 99 copies, or cause a massive paper jam and then leave.

2. Say "Beep, Beep" when a large person takes a step backwards.

3. Whatever somebody says, reply "that's what you think."

4. Write SUBSTANDARD SERVICE on the back of your cheques.

5. Shout out random numbers as loudly as you can, whenever somebody is counting.

6. Wave and honk your horn at passing strangers.

7. Refuse to take a seat in restaurants, just eat complimentary mints.

8. Repeat this conversation as often as you can:

   "Did you SEE that?"

   "What?"

   "Don't worry, it's gone now."

9. End memos in mid-sentence at the bottom of the page.

10. Ask people their gender.

11. Staple pages in all four corners.

12. Paste health warnings about caffeine above the coffee percolator.

13. Skip everywhere you go. Whistling constantly is a nice touch, especially in libraries.

14. Add "according to the Good Book" at the end of all your sentences.

15. Specify that your drive-through order is "to eat in."

16. Sing along at the opera.

17. Try on other people's coats in the cloakroom.

18. Play the William Tell Overture on a comb. When you've virtually finished, announce "Damn, I messed it up" and start again at the beginning.

19. When answering the telephone, ask people to speak up because you can't see too well.

20. Never miss a chance to pick your nose.

after and inspired by Liz S.

DUMB JOKE

A young woman and her husband were playing a round of golf. As she teed off at the fifth hole, the wife sliced her ball off the course and into a residential area. There was a loud crash as it broke a large plate glass window pane. After a discussion, they decided to own up and pay for the damage. On reaching the house they found nobody at home, except a large, fat man wearing a turban and sitting on the carpet.

"Is this your house?" called the woman to him through the window.

"No," he replied, "a golf ball came through the window and broke the glass bottle in which I'd been held prisoner for two thousand years."

"Good heavens," she cried, "Are you a genie?"

"Yes, I am," he answered, "and to show my gratitude, I will grant you two wishes. One wish I'll keep for myself."

The wife and her husband agreed on their two wishes . . . one was that the husband have a scratch handicap and the other that their income never fall below $2 million a year. The genie clapped his hands and cried, "Let it be!"

The couple were delighted.

Then the genie said, "Now it's my turn. I've been in that bottle for centuries without any chance to make love. My wish is that this beautiful woman accompanies me upstairs for a few minutes of passion."

The husband and wife decide that after everything he's done for them, they couldn't refuse. The husband settled down to watch T.V. while the genie and his wife went upstairs.

After they were finished, the fat man asked the wife, "How old is your husband?"

"Thirty-eight," she answered.

"Don't you think it's time he grew out of this genie nonsense?" he asked.

KEEP YOUR FEET WET

When you get in a tight place and everything goes against you, till it seems as though you could not hold up a minute longer, never give up then, for that is just the place and time that the tide will turn.

Harriet Beecher Stowe

Fear not that your life shall come to an end, but rather that it shall never have a beginning.

John Henry Newman

UNDERSTANDING LETTERS OF REFERENCE

YOU'LL BE LUCKY TO GET HIM/HER TO WORK FOR YOU: Never did a damn thing for us.

ACTIVE SOCIALLY: Alcoholic.

CHARACTER ABOVE REPROACH: Nobody's caught him/her yet.

QUICK THINKER: Always has a plausible excuse.

SPENDS EXTRA HOURS ON THE JOB:
Hates one or more of following:
wife/husband/kids/parents.

KEEN SENSE OF HUMOR:
Wastes time telling dirty jokes.

LOYAL: Can't find another job.

CONSULTS WITH SUPERVISOR:
Incompetent, needs constant supervision

VERY CREATIVE:
Never does what you ask him/her to do.

STERN DISCIPLINARIAN:
A pain in the butt, hated by all.

AN ANALYST:
Never actually does anything.

METICULOUS: Nit-picker.

SLIGHTLY ABOVE AVERAGE: Not very bright.

SLIGHTLY BELOW AVERAGE: Braindead.

ALERT TO COMPANY DEVELOPMENTS: Gossip.

TACTFUL: Keeps mouth shut.

SHOULD GO FAR: Please, offer him/her the job.

NO LAUGHING MATTER

Are you too serious? It's been reported that the average five-year old laughs 113 times each day. Unfortunately, by the time we are 44, this drops to 11 laughs daily. Read on, and put some laughter back into your sombre day.

BRIGHT IDEAS

A budget is just a way to allow you to worry before you spend money,
as well as afterwards.

Anon

Few things are harder to put up with than the annoyance of a good example.

Mark Twain

The only thing one can do with good advice is to pass it on. It is never of any
use to oneself.

Oscar Wilde

The hope of the world is still in dedicated minorities. The trailblazers in human,
academic, scientific, and religious freedom have always been in the minority.

Dr. Martin Luther King, Jr.

Don't worry that people will steal your ideas. If they are really any good, you'll
be forced to ram them down people's throats.

after Howard Aiken

Man occasionally stumbles on the truth, but most of them pick themselves up
and hurry off as if nothing had happened.

Winston Churchill

If you can't explain it simply, then you don't understand it well enough.

Albert Einstein

I have not failed. I've just found 10,000 ways that don't work.

Thomas Edison

PUZZLES FOR THE CLUELESS

When you throw your cat out of the car window, does it become kitty litter?

How did the fool get that money?

Why is the word "abbreviation" so long?

Do Kamikaze pilots practice?

Do cannibals refuse to eat clowns because they taste funny?

Why do they put expiry dates on sour cream containers?

NOMINEES FOR SELF SACRIFICE
IN HONOUR OF STUPIDITY

Number One

The Pittsburgh man who tried to reach a bird-feeder on the balcony of his apartment by standing on a wheelchair. Unfortunately, this picked up speed, hit the railing and threw him 23 stories to his death.

Number Two

The heavy sleeper, in San Jose who, when awakened by his ringing telephone, reached for it, but instead accidentally grabbed a .38 Special, held it to his ear and blew his brains out.

Number Three

The individual who strapped a JATO (jet-assisted take-off) unit to his car and found, once ignited, it couldn't be turned off. As a result, he made a 300MPH dent in a Californian cliff, leaving behind very impressive skid marks.

Number Four

The unidentified man from the San Francisco area who used his shotgun to break the windshield of a former girlfriend. During the process, the gun discharged, fatally wounding him in the stomach.

Number Five

The six Turkish people who drowned while trying to rescue a chicken from a well. The farmer climbed down first, but was lost when caught in an undercurrent. His twin sisters and a brother, none of whom swam well, also went into the 80 foot well to save him, but were drowned. Two elderly farmers were then lost in a gallant attempt to assist the family. Eventually, the chicken was pulled out. It survived.

Number Six

Police report that in Seattle, a lawyer attempting to demonstrate the safety of windows in a skyscraper, crashed to his death when the pane broke. He had been illustrating the strength of the building's windows to law students visiting his firm by throwing himself against the glass.
His colleagues described him as "one of the best and brightest members of the company."

PASS ME THE ENVELOPE PLEASE: and the winner is........

PICKUPS AND PUTDOWNS

There's nothing I wouldn't go through for you.
Great, let's start with your bank account.

Your place or mine?
Both. I'll go to mine and you go to yours.

Is this seat vacant?
Yes, and so will this one be if you sit down.

What's it like being the most beautiful girl in town?
What's it like being the biggest liar on earth?

I want to give myself to you.
Sorry, I don't accept damaged goods.

I know the way to please a woman.
Good, then please leave me alone.

Your hair color is wonderful.
Thank you. You can find it on aisle four at the supermarket.

Haven't we met someplace else before?
Yes, that's why I come here now.

REALLY SILLY JOKE

A married couple went to the delivery room together. The doctor said he and his partner had invented a machine that could transfer some of the pain of the birth to the infant's father. He asked if they would be willing to try it out and both agreed. The doctor set the controls at 15 percent, explaining that this much labor pain would probably be worse than anything the husband had ever experienced. But as labor progressed, the husband felt fine and told the doctor to transfer 25 percent of the pain. Even at this level he felt great. The doctor checked his pulse and blood pressure and then moved the dial up to 50 percent. Amazingly, the pain was still easy to take, so the would-be father instructed the doctor to give it all to him. Freed of any pain, the wife delivered a fine, healthy baby in near record time. The couple was ecstatic and were able, a few hours later, to leave the hospital together with their child.

Their joy was diminished somewhat by finding the mailman dead in their driveway.

AN EVEN SILLIER JOKE

Jake, a rancher in Oklahoma, refused to wear a seat belt. One day, he noticed a state policeman following behind him, so he decided to put it on.

"Here, honey, take the wheel for a moment," he cried.

She did, but not fast enough and the trooper pulled them over. The officer walked to the truck and said, "I noticed that you weren't using your seat belt."

"You must be mistaken officer," Jake replied. "But don't take my word about it, speak to my wife."

The officer turned his attention to Jake's spouse.

"So, was he buckled up or not, ma'am?" he asked.

"Officer," she said, "I've been married to this man for 25 years and one thing I've learned is this, never question his word when he's drunk."

DON'T ALWAYS PICK ON LAWYERS

Economists work with numbers because they don't have the personality to become accountants.

Anon

Money says more in a moment than an eloquent lover can say in years. Is this why "diamonds are always a girl's best friend?"

Anon

If all economists were laid end to end, they still couldn't reach a conclusion.

Anon

Education: That which discloses to the wise and disguises from the foolish their lack of understanding.

Ambrose Bierce

God made the Idiot for practice, and then He made the School Board.

Mark Twain

An egotist is a person of low taste—more interested in himself than in me.

Ambrose Bierce

There's no fool like an old fool—you can't beat experience.

Jacob Braude

DIFFERENT HAIRSTYLES

Two Women:

Woman 1:	Have you just had your hair done?
Woman 2:	Yes, yes I have. Thanks for noticing.
Woman 1:	Oh! How could I not notice. It's so stylish and modern.
Woman 2:	Do you think so? I mean, really think so? It's not too short or too curly?
Woman 1:	Oh good heavens no! It's absolutely perfect. If only I could get my hair to look like that, but my face is too square. I'm stuck with this dead old mop.
Woman 2:	You can't be serious? You have such an adorable, attractive face. It's ideal for a layer cut—you'd look like a movie star. I'd intended to have one myself, but my neck is too long as it is and I don't need it accentuated.
Woman 1:	What's wrong with your neck? I'd kill for a neck like yours.
Woman 2:	Are you kidding me? Your shoulders are just perfect. Everything you wear drapes so well on you. I, on the other hand, have arms that are too short. If only I had your shoulders, my clothes would fit so much better.

Two Men:

Man 1:	Haircut?
Man 2:	Yeah, yesterday.

WHY AREN'T YOU MARRIED YET?

1. I'm too intelligent.
2. I've always been lucky.
3. My fiancé is on death row.
4. It isn't worth the price of the blood test.
5. I've more than enough laundry to do now.
6. My pay cheque won't support two.
7. I'm still aiming for a crack at the Miss/Mr. America title.
8. Variety is the spice of life.
9. Why aren't you divorced?
10. I'm waiting until I reach your age, if I live that long.

HIS BEST SHOT

Assassination is the extreme form of censorship.

George Bernard Shaw

A life spent making mistakes is not only more honorable but more useful than a life spent doing nothing.

George Bernard Shaw

It is ridiculous for any man to criticize the works of another if he has not distinguished himself by his own performance.

Joseph Addison

REMEMBER

It's beautiful to do nothing all day, and then rest.

Spanish proverb

I am two fools, I know,
For loving, and for saying so
In whining poetry.
But where's the wiseman that would not be I
If she did not deny?

John Donne "The Triple Fool"

BAD LAWYER JOKES

What would you call 40 skydiving lawyers?
Skeet!

Boy was it cold last winter!
How COLD was it?
Well, I saw a lawyer with both hands in his own pockets.

Did you know the Post Office had to recall a recent stamp release featuring great lawyers of the past?
People were spitting on the wrong side.

Santa Claus, the Easter Bunny, an honest lawyer, and a university professor were in the bank when the power failed and the lights went out. When power was restored, somebody had stolen $1000. Why was the case so easy to solve?
Obviously, it was the professor because the other three are mythical.

RANDOM THOUGHTS

I hesitate to recommend alcohol, drugs, violence or insanity to
anybody, but they've always worked for me.

after Hunter S. Thompson

We die once, and for such a long time.

Molière

I hear and I forget.
I see and I believe.
I do and I understand.

Confucius

NAUGHTY JOKE:
NOT FOR BANKERS

A scruffy individual walks into a small bank and says to the teller, "I'm here to
open a &*!!@*!! savings account!"

The teller, somewhat taken aback, replies, "I'm sorry sir, just what did you say?"

"Keep your ears open, damn you! I told you I'm here to open a &*!!@*!!
savings account, and I want it immediately."

"I'm sorry sir," replied the teller, "but this institution doesn't tolerate that kind
of foul language."

With this comment, she goes over to the bank manager and explains the situation.
They both return to the window.

"Now sir," says the manager, "what seems to be your problem?"

"There's no &*!!*@*!! problem," replies the customer. "I just won $60 million
in the lottery and I need to open a **!!& savings account, right now."

"Yes sir, I understand," the manager replies, "and is this &*!!@*! bitch giving
you trouble?"

GOT YA

Police dislike eavesdropping on their radio frequencies. So they broadcast a
message that a flying saucer had crashed in a wood near Tunstall, Yorkshire.
Six very eager alien buffs arrived, only to discover a police squad which cited
them for telecommunications violations.

POLITICALLY INCORRECT DRINKING JOKE

An Irishman, an Englishman and a Scot walk into a public house and each orders a pint. The bartender fills their glasses and sets them down on the top of the bar. Immediately, three flies appear, one landing in each of the drinks.

The Englishman pushes his aside and in a Cambridge accent says, "I can't possibly drink this!"

The Scot shouts, "Git outa me pint," and blows the foam off the top of the drink with the fly in it. He then quickly swills the beer down.

The Irishman picks the fly out of his drink by its wings, glares into its tiny face and bellows, "Spit it out ya son of a bitch! Spit it all out!!!"

WORDS OF WISDOM

When you stop pretending to be somebody, you are somebody.

Anon

If your life turns out exactly as you expected, what was the point of living it?

Anon

When you were born, you cried and the world rejoiced. Make sure that when you die, history doesn't repeat itself.

Anon

Even if you're on the right track, you'll get run over if you just sit there.

Will Rogers

Be braver. Who can cross a chasm in three small jumps?

Anon

When a dog barks at the moon, then it is religion; but when he barks at strangers, it is patriotism!

David Starr Jordan

A life which is not examined is not worth living.

Plato

Did nothing in particular
And did it very well.

W.S. Gilbert, Lord Mountararat

Never, Never, Never Quit

Winston Churchill

INSIGHTS FROM EXPERTS

This 'telephone' has too many shortcomings to be seriously considered as a means of communication. The device is inherently of no value to us.

Western Union memo, 1877

Courage is doing what you're afraid to do. There can be no courage unless you're scared.

Eddie Richenbacker

A word is not a bird; once flown you can never catch it.

Russian proverb

All right everyone, line up alphabetically according to your height.

Casey Stengel

The halo will become a noose if it drops a few inches.

after Farmers Almanac

When whole races and peoples conspire to propagate gigantic mute lies in the interest of tyrannies and shams, why should we care slightly about the trifling lies told by individuals.

Mark Twain

There are people who think that honesty is always the best policy. This is superstition; there are times when the appearance of it is worth six of it.

Mark Twain

FAT CHANCE

Mrs. Jones was terribly overweight but desperately wanted to lose weight for her daughter's wedding, so she went to her doctor.

"Mrs. Jones," he said, "Eat regularly for three days, then skip a day. If you can keep this up for a month, I guarantee you'll lose 10 pounds."

When Mrs. Jones returned a month later, the scales showed she had lost 30 pounds.

"I'm amazed," said the doctor, "You must have followed my instructions religiously."

She nodded and replied, "I'll tell you though, I nearly died by the end of the fourth day."

"So hungry you mean?" asked the doctor.

"No," she replied, "All that skipping."

A FEW USEFUL HINTS

Don't sow wild oats on weekdays and pray for a crop failure on Sundays.

Success is a private affair, failure occurs in full view.

The wages of sin is death, quit before you get paid.

The sooner you fall behind, the longer you have to catch up.

Don't argue with an idiot. Those watching will probably not be able to distinguish between you.

If you can't live with the answer, don't ask the question.

If you need new ideas, read very old books.

Never look backwards, unless that's the way you want to go.

Like any candle, to give light you have to endure heat.

I'M SORRY YOU ASKED

If a book about failures flops, is it a success?

Do cemetery employees always work the graveyard shift?

Is it possible to mis-spell "incorrectly?"

Would a wingless fly be called a walk?

Are there any closet claustrophobics?

A NAUGHTY JOKE

A couple was due to marry in a week. Something was bothering her.

"Darling," she said, "I just have to know how many women you've slept with."

"But dearest," he replied, "why does it matter? You're the one I love, the past is over, the future's ours."

She insisted that she just had to know before they were wed and continued to press the matter. Finally, he said, "Okay, I'll tell you—one, two, three, four, you, six, seven, eight."

SAY, WHAT DO YOU THINK?

What would it be like if people really said everything they were thinking? How long would the average blind date last? About 25 seconds, "Gee, you've got such a big rear end and bad breath." "Don't mention it, I can't stand your boil and yellow teeth. Bye."

To see the World in a grain of sand,
And Heaven in a wild flower,
Hold Infinity in a palm of your hand,
And Eternity in an hour.

William Blake

YOU CAN SAY THAT AGAIN

Sometimes you're the bug, and on other occasions, you're the windshield.

Anon

Sanity is the playground of the unimaginative.

Anon

When you come to a fork in the road, take it.

Yogi Berra

I'd give my right arm to be ambidextrous.

Yogi Berra

Do not use a hatchet to remove a fly from your friend's forehead.

Chinese proverb

All animals are equal, but some animals are more equal than others.

George Orwell

We are looking for someone who is either very embarrassed or very tired.

A spokesperson for the Melbourne, Australia police, describing a suspect who stole drugs that can cause a 5-day erection from an impotence clinic.

I AM A BOMB DISPOSAL OFFICER: WHEN YOU SEE ME RUNNING TRY TO KEEP UP!

Seen on T-shirt

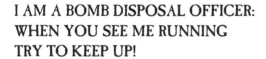

KNOCK, KNOCK

Opportunity is usually difficult to recognize. Don't expect it to beckon you with flashing lights, sirens, beepers and billboards. By then, it's too late.

Anon

Make happy those who are near, and those who are far away will come.

Chinese proverb

GET A LIFE

Life isn't about keeping score. It's not a question of how many friends you have or who accepts you. It's not about this weekend's plans, who you're dating or used to date or even how many people you've dated, or if you haven't been out with anyone. It isn't about who you've kissed. It's not a question of sex, family or how much money they've accumulated, or the kind of automobile you drive. Or where you went to school, college, or church. It's not about beauty or clothes, shoes or the music you like. It's not a question of hair color, black, red, brown, or blonde or if your skin is light or dark. It's not about intelligence, grades or street smarts. It's not about the clubs you join or your sporting achievements. It's not your resume or the cups you've won.

But life is who you love and who you cause pain to. It's about who you make happy. It's about true friendships, starting rumors or spreading gossip. It's about compassion and passing judgements on others. It's about ignoring or helping those in need. It's a question of revenge, fear, ignorance, jealousy and conceit. It's about the cultivation and spreading of hate and love.

Most of all, life is about how you inspire or poison the hearts of others. That's what life is all about.

VIRTUAL REALITY

As a young child, I constantly badgered my mother for information about Santa Claus. I was determined to find out whether or not he was real. She always replied, "Well, you asked for presents and they arrived, didn't they?"
It wasn't until I read the definition of a virtual device, many years later, that I finally understood the full meaning of her answer. The definition reads as follows, "Software or hardware which responds to commands in a manner that is indistinguishable from the real device." My mother was pointing out that Santa Claus was a virtual person, simulated by loving parents, who reacts to the requests of children in a manner that is indistinguishable from that of a real saint.

TWO JOKES NOT TO TELL YOUR LAWYER

A truck driver used to deliberately run down any attorney he saw walking along the highway. One day, he came across a priest whose automobile had broken down, and stopped to offer him a lift.

"Where are you going, Father?" he enquired.

The priest answered, "I was on my way to St. Michael's Church, about six miles down the road."

"No problem. I'd be delighted to take you there, hop in," replied the trucker.

Soon after he'd picked up the priest, the driver noticed a lawyer walking at the side of the road and, out of habit, started to swerve in his direction. At the last moment, he remembered his passenger, so he swerved back, just missing the lawyer. Nevertheless, he was sure he heard a loud THUD! He turned to the priest and enquired what had happened.

The man of the cloth replied, "Well, I could see you were going to miss him, so I swung the door open."

What's the difference between a large pit bull and a female attorney?
Lipstick.

THIS JOKE SUCKS

A preacher visits one of his congregation in the hospital. He sits at the old woman's bedside and starts to talk. Then he notices she has a bowl of peanuts on the night table.

"Do you mind if I take a few peanuts?" he enquires.

"No, be my guest," she answers.

They chat for about an hour and as he rises to leave, the preacher notices he's eaten all the peanuts.

"I'm so sorry," he exclaims, "I only meant to eat a few."

"Oh, that's no problem," she replies, "Since I lost all my teeth, the most I can do is suck off the chocolate."

WAS THAT MY COACH OR TEACHER?

There is nothing more frightful than ignorance in action.

Goethe

BRIGHT IDEAS?

At the peak of the space race in the 1960s, the U.S. National Aeronautics and Space Administration required a ball point pen that was capable of functioning in zero gravity. This problem required extensive research and development to solve, costing roughly $1 million. The Astronaut Pen was also a modestly successful item in the novelty stores. Faced with the same problem, Soviet astronauts were instructed to use pencils.

Seen on a tombstone: SEE, I TOLD YOU I WAS ILL.

My grandmother started to walk 6 miles each day when she reached 75.
She's 83 today and we figure she's probably somewhere in Tibet.

THE BEST OF FRIENDS

Ordinarily he was insane, but he had lucid moments when he was merely stupid.

Heinrich Heine

America is the only country that went from barbarism to decadence without civilization in between.

Oscar Wilde

Childhood: The period of human life intermediate between the idiocy of infancy and the folly of youth—two removes from the sin of manhood and three from the remorse of age.

Ambrose Bierce,
"The Devil's Dictionary"

'DON'T TELL THIS TO A POLICEMAN' JOKE

The police were staking out a very rowdy bar. About ten minutes before closing time, a fellow staggered out and then tried his keys in six cars before finding his own. After several false starts, his car shot out of the lot and disappeared down the highway. The police gave chase, stopped him, and administered the Breathalyzer test. To their amazement, he had a blood alcohol level of 0.0. Looking at the dial he said, "Don't be so surprised, tonight it was my turn to be the designated decoy."

INSPIRATION

A shoe company decided to expand and sent two salesmen to Africa to test the market. After one day, the first wired Head Office, "Coming home, waste of time. Nobody here wears shoes."

Shortly afterwards, the second also wired his boss, "Need more salesmen, nobody wearing shoes here."

WILD ANIMAL STORY

A bum enters a bar and orders whiskey but the bartender says, "No way. You won't be able to pay."

The bum admits, "You've got that right, but if I show you a miracle, will you give it to me?"

At this, the bartender, feeling bored, says, "Agreed, but nothing too dangerous or risque."

The bum pulls a hamster from his tattered coat pocket and puts it on the bar. Immediately, it runs over to the piano and begins to play hymns. It's good, really good. The bartender has to admit, it's a miracle and gives the bum a free whiskey; which he gulps down.

"How about another?" he then asks.

"No way," says the bartender. "Money or another miracle, or no more whiskey."

The bum fishes into his other pocket and pulls out a toad, puts it on the bar and says to it, "Onward Christian Soldiers."

Immediately, the hamster begins playing the hymn and the toad accompanies it in a deep, tuneful voice. It's a wonderful singer. On seeing this, a promoter drinking at the other end of the bar, rushes over and offers the bum $500 for the toad. The bum immediately agrees, the toad changes hands and the promoter leaves with the prize amphibian.

The bartender is amazed and says to the bum, "That's the worst deal I've seen in my life. A religious singing toad like that could be worth millions on the Revival Circuit."

"Don't worry about it," replies the bum, "I needed the money and besides, the hamster is a ventriloquist."

A WILDER ANIMAL STORY

A political prisoner is kept in a dark, damp cell for fifteen years. His only companion is a cockroach, so he spends all his time trying to teach it to recite The Lord's Prayer. After eleven years, it starts to catch on and by the time he is released, it is word perfect.

As soon as his sentence is over, the former prisoner heads to the nearest bar for the drink he's been craving for 15 years. Since he has no money, he expects to have to bargain. He sits on a stool and carefully puts the cockroach down on the bar, ready to demonstrate its unique talking abilities. He then calls over the bartender and says, "Do you see that cockroach?"

"Yes," says the bartender and immediately squashes it flat with a fly swatter. "Don't worry about it, we get them in here all the time. They're not really a problem."

HAVE A GOOD DAY!

A man was tinkering with his motorcycle on his patio. The engine was racing and suddenly the machine slipped into gear, dragging its owner through the patio's glass doors and into the living room. His wife heard the noise, rushed into the room and found him lying bleeding on the carpet. She ran to the telephone, called for medical assistance, and then went down several flights of steps to the road to direct the paramedics to the scene. After the "mechanic" had been taken to the hospital, his wife started to clear up the mess, pushing the motorcycle outside, sweeping up the broken glass, and blotting up spilled gasoline from the carpet. When she had finished, she threw the paper towels into the toilet.

A couple of hours later, her husband limped home, heavily bandaged and badly bruised. Looking at his damaged motorcycle and the destroyed patio doors, he went into the toilet for a smoke to calm his nerves. After taking a few drags of the cigarette, he threw the butt between his legs into the toilet bowl.

Instantly, there was a loud explosion as the gasoline ignited, blowing him off his throne. His wife, who had been making dinner in the kitchen, ran into the bathroom and found her husband badly burned around the groin and buttocks. Again, she ran to the telephone to call for help.

The same ambulance crew quickly arrived, loaded her husband onto a stretcher and began carrying him down the stairs. While they were doing this, one of them asked the wife how her husband had managed to burn himself so badly. Naturally, she told him about the gasoline in the toilet. First one, then all of the crew started laughing, the stretcher tipped and the husband fell out and down the remaining steps, breaking both his legs.

MILKING IDEOLOGIES, FOR WHAT THEY'RE WORTH

FEUDALISM

You have two cows. The lord of the manor sleeps with your bride, leaves you to look after the cows, and takes most of their milk.

SOCIALISM

You have two cows. The government gives them to sheep farmers who put them in a barn with everyone else's cows. You must look after chickens the government has confiscated. In return, you are supplied with the eggs and milk the regulations allow you to need.

FASCISM

You have two cows. The government shoots the one that is genetically impure and hires you to take care of the other. You are permitted to buy milk.

CAMBODIAN COMMUNISM

You have two cows. The government shoots you and takes them.

REPRESENTATIVE DEMOCRACY

You have two cows. Your neighbors elect somebody to tell you who can have the milk.

BUREAUCRACY

You have two cows. The government tells you when, what and how to feed them. It then pays you not to milk one and pours the milk from the other down the drain. It sets up a committee to examine the milk shortage. You must fill in several forms explaining why you failed to meet your pork quota.

CAPITALISM

You have two cows. You sell one to a neighbor and buy a bull.

SURREALISM

You have a goat and an elephant. The government requires you to take violin lessons.

SENSE AND SENSITIVITY

It isn't the mountains that wear you down, it's the grain of sand in your shoe.

Anon

Moderation is a fatal thing. Nothing succeeds like excess.

Oscar Wilde

Don't feel bad if someone calls you mean; feel bad if you are mean.

Spanish proverb

DEFINITIONS

DATING: Spending your money, time and energy to find out about somebody you don't really like and will dislike much more in the future.

EASY: A woman whose morals are those of a man.

EYE CONTACT: How a woman communicates her interest in a man. Many women have problems looking directly into men's eyes, largely because their own eyes are not located in their chests.

NYMPHOMANIAC: A woman with a greater sexual appetite than he has.

SOBER: A state in which it is almost impossible to fall in love.

LAW OF RELATIVITY: How attractive others look is inversely proportional to the attractiveness of your date.

LOVE AT FIRST SIGHT: What happens when two horny but not very selective people meet.

IRRITATING HABITS: What those cute little qualities turn into in a few months.

WHO SAID THAT?

I knew my job was going to the dogs, so I quit the fire hydrant factory.

I killed all my buddies playing tarot card poker one night when I got a straight flush.

I changed my dog's name in case I spilled Spot remover on him and he disappeared.

My neighbors are so dumb they can't find a way out of their circular driveway.

My hobby is collecting sea shells. I hide them on beaches all around the world. You may have seen some of them.

FAMILY TREES

Vincent Van Gogh had many relatives. Genealogists have traced several of the lesser known members of his family tree. These, and their occupations are listed below for art lovers.

The grandfather who moved to Yugoslavia.	- U. Gogh
The great-great-granddaughter who danced up a storm.	- Go Gogh
The really mean sister.	- Please Gogh
The brother who liked prunes.	- Gotta Gogh
His very dizzy aunt.	- Verti Gogh
The daughter who moved to Illinois.	- Chica Gogh
His magician son.	- Wherediddy Gogh
The cousin who spent his holidays in Mexico.	- Amee Gogh
His aunt who was an ornithologist.	- Flamin Gogh

and last, but not least

His father who drove a stage coach.	- Wells Far Gogh

When you read this, please don't say, "What's this ear?"

THE WORST JOKE EVER RECEIVED IN EMAIL

A duck enters a convenience store and asks the manager, "Do you have any strawberries?"

"No, we don't," replies the manager. "They're out of season."

The duck leaves.

The next morning, the duck is back and asks the manager again, "Do you have any strawberries?"

Once again the manager answers, "No, we don't."

A day later, in walks the duck and asks the same question. The manager angrily replies, "Look, ask me that question again Daffy and I'm going to nail you to the floor by your webbed feet."

A day later, the duck returns and asks the manager, "Do you have any nails in stock?"

"No," replies the manager, "we don't."

"Great! In that case, do you have any strawberries?" asks the duck.

ANOTHER WILD ANIMAL JOKE

Three moles lived in a mole hill; a mommy mole, a daddy mole and a little baby mole. Now this hill was situated in a field close to a country farm.

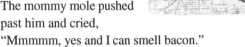

One fine morning, the daddy mole poked his head out of their hole and said, "Mmmmm, I smell freshly baked pancakes."

The mommy mole pushed past him and cried, "Mmmmm, yes and I can smell bacon."

Now the little baby mole tried to squeeze his way out of the hill but couldn't because his parents were blocking the tunnel. He began to sniff anyway and cried, "All I can smell back here is molasses."

Thanks Geoff

LONG LOST FRIEND

George and Alan hadn't seen each other since their college days. When they accidentally met at a ball game, they spent most of the match trying to fill in the gap with details about their lives.

When the game was over, Alan invited George to come over, later in the week, to meet his wife and family.

"Sure," George replied. "What's the address?"

Alan gave it to him and then said, "There's plenty of parking at the back of the apartment. Leave your car there and then go around to the front door. Kick it until it opens, go to the elevator and press the button with your left elbow. Go up to the eighth floor. Turn right, walk down the hall to apartment 809. Then press the bell with your right elbow and I'll open the door for you."

"Okay," said George. "I've got all that. But . . . what's all this kicking doors and elbowing buttons about?"

"Well," replied Alan, "you're not coming empty-handed are you?"

AN OLD JOKE

An old lady was siting at a park bench reading a book when her thoughts were interrupted by an elderly gentleman.

"I'll bet you can't guess my age, " he challenged.

She slowly raised her eyes and said, "Take off your shirt."

He complied. She then commanded, "Turn around."

After carefully looking him over, she continued, "Take off your undershirt and turn around again."

This he did.

"One more thing," she said, "Take off your shoes and socks, run around that tree over there and come back."

This the old man did with enthusiasm.

"You're 95!" she said with confidence.

He was amazed and asked, "That's incredible, how did you know?"

"That's easy," she replied, "You told me this morning."

THEY COULD BE RIGHT

Men are often capable of greater things than they perform.

Horace Walpole

Action may not always bring happiness; but there is no happiness without action.

Benjamin Disraeli

Who dares nothing, need hope for nothing.

Henri Bergson

When two men in business always agree, one of them is unnecessary.

William Wrigley, Jr.

There is no conversation more boring than the one when everybody agrees.

Michel de Montaigne

Sometimes one pays most for the things one gets for nothing.

Albert Einstein

Nothing's beautiful from every point of view.

Horace

SELECTED BUMPER STICKERS

How can I miss you if you won't go away?

I break to annoy you.

I'm not as think you as drunk am I.

Time keeps everything from happening together.

I love cats . . . they taste just like lamb.

Out of my mind. Back in ten minutes.

I exercise by pushing my luck daily.

Sometimes I wake up grumpy; other times I let him sleep late.

Reality is a crutch for those who can't handle drugs.

OK, who stopped payment on my reality cheque?

I don't care if you tell me to stuff it—I'm a taxidermist.

Horn damaged. Watch out for finger.

My IQ test results were negative.

Be kind to your kids. They'll select your retirement home.

Beauty is in the eyes of the beer holders.

We have pride. You have vanity.

No dates outside my species.

Women who want equality lack ambition.

SHAGGY DOG STORY

A blind man makes his way into a bar with the aid of his seeing eye dog. He walks into the center, picks the dog up by its collar and swings it around his head. The bartender is amazed at this and shouts, "Hey! Whaddaya think you're trying to do?!"

The blind man stops, puts the dog down and says, "Don't worry. I was just looking around."

PRESIDENTIAL CLARIFICATION

If I said anything which implies that I think that we didn't do what we should have done, given the choices we faced at the time, I shouldn't have said that.

Bill Clinton

The President has kept all of the promises he intended to keep.

Clinton aide George Stephanopolous speaking on Larry King Live

ADDENDUM TO THE PERIODIC TABLE

ELEMENT: Woman
SYMBOL: Woe
ATOMIC WEIGHT: 125 (more or less)

PHYSICAL PROPERTIES: Round, soft. Boils easily but may be frigid at times. Can melt if treated with care but become very bitter if misused.

CHEMICAL PROPERTIES: Has strong affinity for precious metals and stones, especially diamonds. Slightly green when compared with younger specimens.

USAGE: Ornamental, with some economic, political and social applications. High capacity to disintegrate wealth. One of the most powerful financial reducing agents known.

ELEMENT: Man
SYMBOL: XY
ATOMIC WEIGHT: 175 +/- 50

PHYSICAL PROPERTIES: Often quite dense and sometimes very flaky.

CHEMICAL PROPERTIES: Attempts to bond with Woe at every opportunity, especially with younger samples.

USAGE: Value typically overestimated. Major source of methane and hot air.

CAUTION: In the absence of Woe, this element collects dirt and begins to smell bad.

INSULTS FOR EVERYDAY USE

Not the sharpest knife in the drawer.

Dived into the gene pool while the lifeguard was off duty.

Room temperature IQ.

A gross ignoramus—144 times as gross as an ignoramus.

A photographic memory, but no film in the camera.

A prime candidate for natural deselection.

Medical school would reject his body for dissection.

During evolution, his ancestors didn't make the control group.

Her family tree suffered from root rot.

Has two brains; one missing and the other searching for it.

If she were any more stupid, we'd water her twice a week.

If he asks for a penny for his thoughts, demand change.

One neuron short of a synapse.

Takes 2.5 hours for him to watch "60 Minutes."

after Leone

JUST NUTS

I've been paying a psychiatrist $150 an hour, three times a week, for five years. Do you think I'm crazy?

• • •

Six months after his marriage to a twenty-eight year old beauty, a rich centenarian mentioned to his physician that his wife was expecting a child.

"That reminds me of a story," smiled the doctor. "I had a patient who was on safari. One night, he was disturbed by a lion's roar. He grabbed what he thought was his gun, ran out of his tent holding his umbrella. Immediately, the lion charged him! Pointing the umbrella, the former patient of mine shot and killed it."

"That's impossible," cried the old man, "Somebody else's bullet must have been responsible."

"Exactly," replied the doctor.

MALE BASHING

1. The best reason to get rid of a man is a health reason: you're sick of him.

2. If you still believe that the way to a man's heart is through his stomach, try lowering your aim.

3. Look for a young man. You may as well, none of them are mature.

4. The woman's work that is never finished is that which she asked her husband to do.

5. If one man can wash 25 plates in 30 minutes, how many can five men wash in 4 hours? None, they'll order pizza and watch football.

6. Scientists have just discovered something capable of doing the jobs of three men—a woman.

7. Men's brains have the same problems as prisons—too many men per cell.

8. There are only two four letter words that men object to—"don't" and "stop", unless of course, they're used together.

9. Men are animals—messy, insensitive and with a capacity for violence, but they can be great pets, once house-trained.

10. How many men does it take to screw in a light bulb? Seven. One to screw in the bulb and six to talk about hockey.

I WISH I'D BEEN THERE

1. Raptor's confrontation with Tyrannosaurus Rex.

2. The painting of the leaping bison at Altamira (c 30,000 BC)

3. The discovery and perfection of fire.

4. The birth of Christ, or The Last Supper (c. 29 A.D.).

5. The signing of the Declaration of Independence in Philadelphia (July 4, 1776).

6. Abraham Lincoln delivering the Gettysburg address.

7. The first airplane flight by Orville and Wilbur Wright at Kitty Hawk, N.C.

8. My parents meeting for the first time.

9. Hitler's last day in the bunker (April 30, 1945).

10. Kennedy assassination in Dallas (November, 1963).

And, an aside:

11. As a spectator instead of a participant . . . my own birth (November 17, 1962).

THINGS ARE ON THE WAY DOWN

Heaven is getting too crowded and so it is decided to send newcomers back to earth, if they have had exceptionally bizarre deaths. Saint Peter conducts the necessary interviews at the Pearly Gates. Three men arrive together, but there is only room for two to enter. So the Saint asks the first how he died.

"Well," is the reply, "I was working at the office when I received a telephone call from the janitor of the apartment building where I lived. He told me that my wife was fooling around again with one of our neighbors. So I raced home, caught her in bed but there was no sign of any boy-friend. I looked everywhere, but I couldn't find the guy. Finally, I opened the window and there was the fool hanging from our 12th floor balcony. I smashed his fingers with a hammer and he fell, but on the way down, he managed to grab the balcony on the floor below. In my rage, I picked up our refrigerator and dropped it on his head. Unfortunately, its electrical cord wrapped around my right ankle and pulled me over, killing me.

"I must admit that's a bizarre death," says Saint Peter. "Now how about you?" he asks the second man.

"I was cleaning the windows on the 13th floor of this apartment block when I slipped on my bar of soap," came the reply. "Luckily, although I fell over the balcony, I managed to save myself by catching onto the one below. Then this idiot opened his balcony window and instead of helping me in, he smashed my fingers with a hammer. Again, my luck held and I managed to grab the balcony on the 11th floor. But, and I still can't believe it, the swine on the 12th floor tossed his refrigerator at me, knocking me off to my death."

"Bizarre, very bizarre indeed," says Saint Peter. "Let's hear what happened to you," he continued, pointing to the third in line.

"Well, I was visiting a friend and decided to climb into her refrigerator to cool off when....."

MY MISTAKE

They laughed at Joan of Arc, but she went right ahead and built it.

Gracie Allen

I'm in shape. Round's a shape, isn't it?

Anon

HOCKEY JOKE

Heaven was getting crowded, again, and so it was decided to let only the very brave through the Pearly Gates. Saint Peter, as usual, was in charge of entry.

"Well," he said to the first man to arrive after the decision had been made, "What was the bravest thing you ever did?"

The man replied, "I was a hockey referee and was in charge of a game in the Forum between the Montreal Canadiens and the Philadelphia Fliers. The score was tied with 30 seconds left in the third period. Philadelphia had been by far the better team, but Montreal's goal keeper had been outstanding. Then there was a pile-up in the Montreal goal. The puck only half-crossed the line, but since Philadelphia deserved the win, I signalled a goal."

"That," said Saint Peter, "was a very brave thing to do, but I'll need confirmation from our records."

The Saint re-entered Heaven, leaving the referee waiting outside. Two minutes later Peter returned, shaking his head. "I'm sorry," he said, "we have no record of that event. When did it happen?"

"Well," answered the referee, "I guess it must have been about three minutes ago."

TWO MEAN JOKES: FOR REPUBLICANS ONLY

Bill and Hillary are eating dinner at a high quality restaurant. Their waiter tells them that the specials for the evening are chicken almondine and smoked salmon.

"The chicken sounds good to me; I'll have that," says Hillary.

The waiter smiles, nods and enquires, "And what about the vegetable?"

"Oh, he'll have the salmon," Hillary replies.

• • •

President Clinton returns from his vacation in Arkansas. As he leaves Air Force One, he's carrying two pigs under his arms. The honor guardsman steps forward at the bottom of the stairway and remarks, "Great pigs, Mr. President."

Clinton replies, "These, my man, are genuine Arkansas Razor-Back Hogs. I got the right one for Chelsea and the left one for Hillary. So what do you think now?"

The honor guardsman replies, "Nice trade, Sir. Nice trade."

I DIDN'T KNOW THAT

The dot completing the letter "i" is called a tittle.

Samuel Clemens (aka Mark Twain) was born on a day in 1835 when Haley's Comet came into view and died in 1910 as it reappeared.

Nutmeg injected intravenously is extremely poisonous.

Three of the six men who played the Three Stooges were brothers; Moe, Curly, and Shemp.

Ohio, although listed as the 17th state in the United States, is technically only the 47th. Congress forgot to vote on a resolution to admit it to the Union until August 7, 1953.

If you have three quarters, four dimes and four pennies, while you have $1.19, you still can't make change for a dollar.

The volume of the Moon is the same as that of the Pacific Ocean.

The commonest name on earth is Mohammed.

Spot, Data's cat on Star Trek: The Next Generation, was a role played by six feline actors.

The longest US highway is Route 6. This begins in Cape Cod, Massachusetts and ends in Bishop, California.

Underground is the only word in the English language beginning and ending with und.

The housefly hums in the middle octave, key of F.

Tigers have striped skin, not simply striped fur.

For most advertisements, including those in newspapers and magazines, watches are shown at 10:10.

Facetious and abstemious contain all the vowels in order.

Al Capone's business card claimed he was a used furniture dealer.

No two lions possess the same pattern of whiskers, so it can be used for identification like a fingerprint.

Grapes put into a microwave oven will explode.

HOW MUCH WOOD WOULD A WOODPECKER PECK?

Two large trees, side by side in the forest, notice a small sapling growing close by. One says to the other, "Is that a son of a beech or a son of a birch?"

The other looks it over and can't make up his mind. At that moment, a woodpecker lands in one of their branches and they decide to seek his advice.

"Woodpecker, we respect your opinion, you're the tree expert. Can you tell us whether that young sapling is a son of a beech or a son of a birch?" they asked.

The woodpecker swoops down to the small tree and starts banging away. Then he flies back and says, "I'm afraid it's not a son of a beech or a son of a birch. That dear friends, is the best piece of ash I ever put my pecker into."

JUST FOR THE MILITARY RECORD

His men follow him anywhere, out of curiosity.

This young officer has delusions of adequacy and completes every task to her own satisfaction.

In my last report, I claimed he had reached rock bottom. Unfortunately, since then, he has been digging.

He has youth's wisdom coupled with the energy of the elderly.

He would be out of his depth in a puddle.

This officer behaves like a gyroscope, spins around at a frantic speed but goes nowhere.

Whenever she opens her mouth, she only manages to replace one foot with another.

This officer is more of a definitely won't-be than a has-been.

She sets very low standards and than fails to achieve them.

Not breeding material.

His presence here is depriving some village of its idiot.

SELF-HELP

He who has so little knowledge of human nature as to seek happiness by changing anything but his own disposition will waste his life in fruitless efforts.

Samuel Johnson

Everyone thinks of changing the world, but no one thinks of changing himself.

Tolstoy

A LITTLE THOUGHT

One ought, every day at least, to hear a little song, read a good poem, see a fine picture, and, if it were possible, to speak a few reasonable words.

Goethe

Where there is an open mind, there will always be a frontier.

Charles F. Kettering

The end of all knowledge should be a virtuous action.

Phillip Sydney

The worth of a book is what you can carry away from it.

James Bryce

The greater part of our happiness or misery depends on our dispositions, and not on our circumstances. We carry the seeds of the one or the other about with us in our minds wherever we go.

Martha Washington

Every living creature that comes in to the world has something allotted him to perform, therefore he should not stand an idle spectator of what others are doing.

Sarah Kirby Timmer

Life is what happens to you while you are making other plans.

A.J. Marshall

I either want less corruption, or more chance to participate in it.

Ashleigh Brilliant

Excess on occasion is exhilarating. It prevents moderation from acquiring the deadening effect of a habit.

W. Somerset Maugham

Better murder an infant in its cradle than nurse an unacted desire.

William Blake

Ah, but a man's reach should exceed his grasp—or what's a Heaven for?

Robert Browning

Given the choice between the experience of pain and nothing, I would choose pain.

William Faulkner

WORDS OF WISDOM

No duty is more urgent than that of
returning thanks.

Ambrose of Milan

Laugh and the world laughs with you,
Weep and you weep alone,
For the sad old earth must borrow its mirth,
But has trouble enough of its own.

Ella Wheeler Wilcox

It is better to be alone than in bad
company.

George Washington

Two things I hate: people who can't count.

Bill S.

'DON'T TELL THIS ONE TO AN ENGINEER' JOKE

A physician, a priest and an engineer were playing behind a very slow group of golfers.

Engineer: "What's their problem? They've been holding us up for a least 20 minutes."

Physician: "I can't believe such incompetence."

Priest: "Here comes the greenskeeper. Let's see if there's anything that he can do."

Priest: "Hi Bill. What's the problem with that group in front of us? They're very slow aren't they?"

Bill: "Yes, I'm afraid they are. But, they're blind firefighters who lost their vision fighting our clubhouse fire a couple of years ago, so they play here for free, any time they like."

The group was silent for a few moments.

Priest: "That's terrible. Very, very sad. Sunday, my congregation will say a special prayer for them."

Physician: "You do that, but I'm going to contact an ophthalmologist I know. He's the best, maybe he can do something."

Engineer: "Those guys should play at night."

WHAT HAPPENS WHEN TWO PEOPLE WITH THE SAME MAJOR BREAK UP

PSYCHOLOGY: The girl accused her former boyfriend of using her as a mother substitute. He agreed.

WOMEN'S STUDIES: "HE did it, didn't he!"

JOURNALISM: Today an era closed. Jack, a 19 year old white male and Jill, an 18 year old white female, decided enough was enough, and so put an end to their 3 week relationship. Who knows what . . . .

PHYSICS: Both accepted the reality that relationships are not of infinite length.

BIOLOGY: "You wanted to get into my genes!"

ARCHAEOLOGY: One digs up the past, the other tries to bury it.

SOCIOLOGY: Each claimed to be oppressed within the relationship.

BUSINESS: Both decided that any profits from the relationship were outweighed by its costs.

GEOGRAPHY: Both decided to separate to avoid boundary disputes.

ANATOMY: "I don't think your body cuts it!"

ECONOMICS: Relationship supply outstripped demand.

ENGLISH: The breaking up letters were immaculate. Each had an introduction, thesis, body, and conclusion, but neither said anything intelligible or possessed true insight.

EDUCATION: Both accepted that the relationship had been a learning experience.

ELECTRICAL ENGINEERING: The break-up came as a shock to both, despite the relationship's positives and negatives.

ITALIAN: "Mama Mia!"

ARCHITECTURE: "The relationship just didn't have a solid foundation."

JEWISH STUDIES: "OY! You should feel so guilty!"

PHILOSOPHY: If two people break up in a deserted dorm, but there are no other witnesses, are they truly no longer a couple?

ZOOLOGY: They mated like banshees but lacked an adequate grasp of communication skills.

CHEMISTRY: "We had a bad reaction."

LAW: They each sued for breach of their pre-dating agreement.

EXCUSES AND INSIGHTS

They're multipurpose. Not only do they put the clips on, but they take them off.

> *Spokesperson for a large engineering company*
> *explaining why it charged the US Air Force*
> *nearly $1000 for a pair of ordinary pliers.*

When more and more people are thrown out of work, unemployment results.

> *Calvin Coolidge*

THINK ABOUT THIS FOR A MOMENT

The scalded cat fears even cold water.

> *Thomas Fuller*

There's nothing like desire to prevent the things one says from having any resemblance to the things in one's mind.

> *Marcel Proust*

The morality of an action depends on the motive from which we act.

> *Samuel Johnson*

A woman inserted an advertisement in the newspaper classifieds. It simply read, "Husband wanted." She received hundreds of replies. They all said exactly the same thing, "You're welcome to mine."

> *Anon*

Religion is verily the chief instrument for the establishment of order in the world and of tranquility amongst its peoples . . . The greater the decline of religion, the more grievous the waywardness of the ungodly. This cannot but lead in the end to chaos and confusion.

> *Baha' Allah*

It's like deja vu all over again.

> *Yogi Berra*

Say it with roses, say it with mink, but don't forget, never say it with ink.

> *Anon*

DON'T HOLD YOUR BREATH

Ten Things a Woman NEVER Says:

1. That swim suit really makes your figure look wonderful! Please, keep my husband company while I take a dip.

2. That woman and I are wearing the same dress. We must have similar tastes. I'll go over and introduce myself.

3. I'm happy for him. His new girlfriend is far nicer looking than I am, and sweet natured as well.

4. When I don't control the remote, I act like a bitch.

5. He was earning more than I was, so I broke up with him.

6. I'm so tired of doctors, lawyers and professors, I've decided to date a golden-hearted waiter.

7. We're redecorating the kitchen and he keeps pestering me to suggest a color scheme.

8. Talk, talk, talk. Can't he stop burdening me with details of his emotions?

9. Why can't I find somebody who will treat me like a sex object for a night of carefree fun?

10. My butt doesn't just look too fat, it is too fat.

Ten Things a Man NEVER Says:

1. I'm tired of beer.

2. I just can't stop fantasizing about Dr. Ruth's body.

3. Does my butt look fat to you?

4. Yours is definitely longer than mine.

5. Those huge, jacked-up trucks are positively ridiculous.

6. There's nothing I'd like to do more than spend a quiet evening at home with your mother, watching a video about the spiritual benefits of suffering.

7. I just gave away my tools. Nothing I make is ever up to standard, anyway.

8. Let's go to the movies, I feel like a good cry.

9. I'm definitely against the trend of bralessness in beautiful younger women.

10. Our team lost 12-1, but we tried hard and it was a learning experience for us all. That's what really counts.

HAVE YOU HAD ENOUGH?

Do you lose arguments with lamp posts and other inanimate objects?

Do you grab hold of the lawn to stop yourself slipping off the earth?

Is your employment forcing you to restrict your drinking hours?

Is there blood in your alcohol stream?

Do you keep injuring your head on the toilet?

Do you drink all your meals?

Does your home address change while you're in the bar?

Are your sons named Hops and Barley?

Do mosquitoes become intoxicated after attacking you?

At AA meetings, do you suggest "Let's all have a drink"?

Is your idea of cutting back to put less salt on your peanuts?

Does the whole bar greet you by name?

NOW THIS IS A BAD DAY

In 1986, a New York man parked his van on a street that had a downhill grade. After completing his trip to the doctor's, he found his car wedged between a coal truck and another van. As a result, he was completely unable to get out of the parking spot. Thinking for a while, he decided that if he released the coal truck's emergency brake, it would roll forward down the hill and provide him with enough room to pull his car out of its cramped parking spot. Fortunately, the truck was not locked so he climbed on board, but was confronted by a whole array of levers. Unsure which of them controlled the hand brake, he pulled the nearest and instantly buried his own van under six tons of coal.

CHUCKLES

"Am I the first boy you've kissed?"
"I'm not sure. When you were younger, did you have a beard?"

"Does insanity run in your family?"
"Yes, doctor. My husband thinks he's the boss."

"I broke up with my boyfriend last night. He wanted to get married, and I didn't want him to."

"How's your wife's dieting working out?"
"Great. Last night she disappeared completely."

"The psychiatrist has really helped me get over my phobia. I used to be too afraid to answer the telephone when it rang. Now I answer it, whether it rings or not."

"Why do you refuse to divorce your husband?"
"What, after all he's done to me!? Why should I make that swine happy?"

"Waiter, what's the difference between the $5 steak and the $10 steak?"
"Exactly $5, Sir."

"Did you go to Paris for your holidays?"
"I'm not sure, my wife bought the tickets."

WEDDED BLISS JOKE

A newly wed couple went to visit the doctor. After the checkups were finished, the physician took the bride to one side and said, "If you don't follow my instructions, your husband will surely die."

"Every morning, get up early and make him a healthy nutritious breakfast, including fresh hand-squeezed juice, pancakes, and bacon. Let him read the newspaper uninterrupted, whisper words of love in his ear, then send him to work in a wonderful mood with a passionate kiss. At lunch, make him a delicious meal, massage his neck and back, and keep him in a good frame of mind for the rest of the afternoon. Fix him a four course meal for dinner. Eat it by candlelight while you listen to his favorite music. Don't complain about doing all the household chores. Make wild, passionate love several times each week and always act as if you're on a second honeymoon. Satisfy his every whim."

Later, in their car on the way home, the husband asked his wife what the physician had been saying to her. "You're going to die," she answered.

MORE CHUCKLES

"Why did you throw the chair at your husband?"
"Well, your Honor, I couldn't lift the table."

"When I saw you driving through that red light, I guessed 65 at a minimum."
"You're way off base there, officer, it's just this hat that makes me seem older."

"Yesterday, I passed your house."
"Don't think I fail to appreciate it."

"Were you familiar with Ann Jones?"
"Well I tried to be, but she slapped my face."

"I went on the honeymoon by myself. My wife had already been to Niagara Falls."

Bigamy is having one wife too many. Monogamy is the same.

Oscar Wilde

ENVIRONMENTALLY INCORRECT
ENDANGERED SPECIES NEWS

A hiker was exploring the Olympic Mountains but got lost.
For five days, he struggled to find his way back to civilization.
Without food the entire time, he was very hungry. Suddenly,
he spotted a bald eagle on a rock ledge and killed it with a well
thrown stone. He then lit a fire and cooked and ate the bird.

As luck would have it, just as he was finishing eating,
two park rangers, alerted by the smoke, arrested him
for killing a member of an endangered species.
In his court appearance, his lawyer claimed
necessity as a defence, stating that, if he had
not eaten the bald eagle, he might have died of
starvation. After hearing all the evidence, the
judge ruled in the hiker's favor and dismissed
the charges. In his closing statement, the judge
then asked the acquitted man, "Before you are
released, can you tell me something? I've never eaten
a bald eagle, nor will I ever. What did it taste like?"

To which the hiker answered, "Well, I suppose you could say it tasted a
bit like a cross between a spotted owl and a whooping crane."

QUOTE: MISQUOTE?

John Wilkes Booth (next day): "Did the reviews mention me?"

Marlon Brando: "Don't worry, one day I'll be much bigger than Orson Wells."

Al Capone (advice to his son): "Look after friends, punish enemies, and always keep the receipts."

Abraham (at the first circumcision): "Isaac, this will definitely hurt you more than it will hurt me."

Harry Foster: The word 'impossible' isn't in my dictionary. In fact, everything from 'help' to 'minute' appears to be missing.

Attila the Hun (talking to his troops): "Gentlemen, remember this is a simple looting, not an uncivilized massacre."

Ludwig von Beethoven: "Who cares about the critics? I never listen to a word they say."

Alexander Graham Bell (inventing telephone sex): "Mrs. Watson. Is your husband still out on that errand? Good, come here. I want you. Bad, real bad!"

Eve (easily impressed, first woman): "Three inches! Wow, that's huge!"

GOOD REASONS FOR NOT BEING AT WORK

I'm taking the day off to stalk my former boss, who had me fired for taking the day off.

This morning I accidentally mixed my laxative with my anti-depressant. I'm sitting on the John, but feeling good about it.

My voices told me to spend the day awaiting further instructions.

I just discovered that there was a mix-up at the hospital when I was born. Legally, I shouldn't come in to work because my employee records contain false personal data.

It's Easter and my stigmata are in full flow.

I have a rare case of 3-day Ebola bizarre.

The dog swallowed my car keys, so we have to hitchhike to the veterinary clinic.

QUOTATIONS TO REMEMBER

Independence is the only gauge of human virtue and value. What a man is and makes of himself is not what he has or hasn't done for others.

Ayn Rand

Don't go where the path leads, rather go where there are no paths and create a new trail.

Anon

Remember, even when you fall flat on your face, you must move forward.

Anon

We must all plant trees we'll never sit under.

Anon

If a man does not keep pace with his companions, perhaps it is because he hears a different drummer.

Henry David Thoreau

Audacter calumniare semper aliquid haeret (Slander boldly, something always sticks).

Anon

Women with pasts interest men . . . they hope history will repeat itself.

Mae West

Marriage is a great institution, but I'm not ready for an institution.

Mae West

Sometimes a cigar is just a cigar.

Sigmund Freud

I am a greater believer in luck and I find the harder I work, the more I have of it.

Stephen Leacock

CHINESE INSULT

May you live in interesting times.

SAY THAT AGAIN

I've gone out to find myself. If I happen to return before I get back, please hold me until I get there.

Anon

GET MOVING

Each morning as the African sun rises, a gazelle wakes up. It recognizes that it must be able to outrun the fastest lion or it will be killed and eaten. Every morning as the African sun rises, a lion awakes with the knowledge that, unless it wants to starve, it must outrun the slowest gazelle. WHEN THE SUN COMES UP, YOU'D BETTER BE ABLE TO RUN.

GOLDEN OLDIES

Anyone who stops learning is old, whether at 20 or 80. Anyone who keeps learning stays young. The greatest thing in life is to keep your mind young.

Henry Ford

The average person puts only 25 percent of his energy and ability into his work. The world takes off its hat to those who put more than 50 percent of their capacity, and stands on its head for those few and far between souls who devote 100 percent.

Andrew Carnegie

Genius without education is like silver in the mine.

Ben Franklin

The best thing to do behind a person's back is pat it.

Anon (but nice)

A criminologist is a person with his feet planted firmly in mid air.

Anon

Don't be humble, you're not that great.
Golda Meir

If you want to be respected by others the great thing is to respect yourself.

Dostoevsky

The trouble with most of us is that we would rather be ruined by praise than saved by criticism.

Norman Vincent Peale

YOU DIDN'T KNOW THAT

The Eisenhower Interstate system requires that one in every five miles of highway must be straight, so they can be used for aircraft to land on.

The Boston University Bridge, on Commonwealth Avenue in Boston, Massachusetts is the only location on earth where a ship can sail under a train that is passing under an automobile driving under an airplane.

Cats have approximately ten times as many vocal sounds as dogs.

Our eyes are always the same size after birth but our ears and nose always keep growing.

Camel's milk will not curdle.

Jeep is derived from the army abbreviation G.P. (General Purpose) vehicle.

Since 1896, when the modern Olympics began, only Australia and Greece have competed in every Games.

February 1865 is the only month in recorded history that did not have a full moon.

The great cruise liner, Queen Elizabeth II, can move only about 6 inches on a gallon of diesel fuel.

The only author to have a book in every Dewey-decimal category is Isaac Asimov.

The two largest landowners in New York City are the Catholic Church and Columbia University.

Scissors were invented by Leonardo Da Vinci.

Babies have no knee caps. These develop when the child is between 2 and 6 years old.

The highest point in Pennsylvania is lower than the lowest point in Colorado.

Parts of Ontario, Canada are farther south than parts of California.

Only one person in every 2 billion will live to be 116 years old or greater.

Cats' urine glows under blacklight.

There are two credit cards for each person in the United States.

Screeched is the longest one-syllable word in English.

If you straighten a coat hanger, it will be 44 inches long.

Canada is an aboriginal word which means "Big Village."

Byte is a contraction of "by eight" and pixel of either "picture cell" or "picture element."

The average ear of corn consists of eight-hundred kernels in sixteen rows.

BRITISH WISDOM

There is nothing so exhilarating as to be shot at and missed.

Winston Churchill

If you want a picture of the future, imagine a boot stamping on a human face . . . forever.

George Orwell

THE UNKNOWN THINKER

Suicide is the extreme example of taking one's self too seriously.

Anon

A goal without a date is merely a wish.

Anon

The past was erased, the erasure was forgotten, the lie became truth.

George Orwell

If A equals success, then the formula is A equals X plus Y plus Z. X is work. Y is play. Z is keep your mouth shut.

Albert Einstein

To his dog, every man is Napoleon. This accounts for the unwavering popularity of dogs.

Anon

WHY? TELL ME WHY

If you tell a man that there are 400 billion stars in the sky, he'll believe it. But if you tell him to stay off the bench because you've just painted it, he just has to touch it.

How much deeper would the ocean be without sponges?

If "Con" is the opposite of "Pro", then what is the inverse of PROGRESS?

Is infancy to infants what adultery is to adults?

Why are HAMBURGERS all made out of BEEF?

Why doesn't glue stick to the inside of the tube?

Shouldn't we cure pigs before they die?

A MAN WITH AN ATTITUDE

George was a positive thinker, who always had a kind remark or something nice to say to everybody. When anyone asked him how he was doing, he would answer, "If I were any better, I'd have to be twins."

George was a natural manager. Sales clerks would follow him from store to store, as his career moved him up the ladder of success. They did this because George was a motivator who made everyone around him happy. If things went wrong, George didn't complain, he told his employees to use it as a learning experience and search for its positive aspects.

George bothered me a little. I couldn't believe all his bonhomie was for real. Surely, cordiality had its limits. So one day, I asked him about it.

"George," I said. "I don't understand how you can be so happy and friendly the entire time. Why don't you have bad days like everybody else?"

George replied, "Well, every morning when I wake up, I remind myself that I can decide to be in either a good mood, or in a bad one. I always decide good is better. So I choose to be happy and contented. If, during the day, something awful happens, I can choose to be a whining victim, or I can choose to gain from the experience. When people gripe and complain, I can gripe and complain right back, or I can choose to point out to them the positive side of the situation."

"Well," I replied. "That's not easy to keep up."

"Yes, it is," answered George. "Remember, every situation is simply an opportunity to choose. You choose how you will react in all situations, whether someone or something will make you upset or not. It's your choice how you will live your life, happy or sad."

Many times I thought over just what George had told me. Slowly, but surely, I began to take his advice and developed a better attitude. With this improved attitude came promotion and finally my own business. I lost contact with George for a while and then learned he'd been badly wounded. Apparently, he'd been shot by panicking robbers in a hold-up attempt at a bakery he'd been managing.

About six months after the shooting, I met George at a ball game. When I enquired after his health, he replied as usual, "If I were any better, I'd have to be twins."

I began to probe him about the robbery and his shooting.

"Well," he said, "When they wheeled me into that emergency room and I looked up at the faces of the surgeons and nurses, I could see they thought I was a dead man."

"What did you do?" I enquired.

"Well," said George, "One of the nurses shouted questions at me, trying to find out if I was allergic to anything. Yes, I replied. The medics stopped their work for a moment waiting to hear what it was. So I took a deep, deep breath and shouted as loud as I could, BULLETS! They all started to laugh and when they stopped, I said to them, let's get on with it, I'm choosing life. Operate on me if you are sure I'm going to live, not die."

George is back to his old self. Partially because of the skills of the surgeons and nurses it's true, but also because of his attitude. If I learned anything from George, it's this—every day we have the chance to live successfully or not. To make the most of your life, GET AN ATTITUDE.

HEADLINES FOR INTELLECTUALS

Something Went Wrong in Jet Crash, Expert Says.

Lab Reports Fish in Perfect Health, Except Dead.

Miners Refuse to Work After Death.

Court to Try Shooting Defendant.

Peace Hopes Dimmed by War.

New Bridge Held Up by Red Tape.

Obesity Study Looks for Larger Test Group.

Kids Make Nutritious Snacks.

Rotten Wood Replaced by Alumni.

Include Children when Baking Cookies.

Troglodytes

DON'T GAMBLE ON IT

A man entered a casino in Las Vegas and walked to the rear, where the cashier's cage was located. He pulled out a shotgun and demanded a large amount of money. This the cashier reluctantly gave him. The robber then tucked his shotgun under his coat and started to casually walk away. The cashier immediately contacted security, and in moments the thief was surrounded by guards. Anxious not to cause a scare, they began to follow him towards the exit. Realizing he was in deep trouble, the robber decided to play for time and instead of leaving, sat down at a card game. He played several hands, still surrounded by waiting security guards. The game continued without interruption. Suddenly, in an attempt to cause confusion, the robber overturned the table sending chips and cards flying. This enraged the other card players who began beating and kicking him. If security guards had not intervened, he may well have been killed. The thief was taken to hospital on a stretcher and the rest of the players quickly resumed their game.

A WORD FOR THE WISE

I believe we should try harder to make this world a better place for our children. However, I don't think we should do anything for our children's children. After all, our children shouldn't be having sex.

Boxing is like ballet, except there's no music, no choreography and the goal is to cause as much pain to the other dancer as possible.

Whenever I read a great book, it's just as if its author is standing beside me in the room. That's why I never read great books.

Being kept chained to the wall in a deep dungeon is probably not much fun. But on days when there is a bad thunderstorm, you could look up at the sky through the bars of your tiny cell and say "I'm glad that I'm not caught out in that."

Consider the rose. Examine its scent, petals, thorns and stem. While you're doing that, I'll be sorting through your belongings to see if there's anything I really like.

When I die, I hope the epitaph on my gravestone reads "Owed money to almost everybody in town."

If I ruled a country that had been defeated in war, just as I was signing the peace treaty, I'd read it for a minute and then cry, "Hey, wait a minute! We won, didn't we?"

Vampire children are warned never, never to play with wooden stakes.

My geography teacher told me it was frightening just how much of our topsoil we were losing to erosion. But when I told my friends around the camp fire, nobody screamed.

In the Dark Ages, one of the biggest mistakes you could make was to forget to put your armor on when you went down to the corner store.

MEDICAL INSIGHTS TAKEN FROM REAL MEDICAL REPORTS

As she fainted, both her eyes rolled around the office.

She admitted she had been constipated until 1988, when her divorce became final.

Diagnosis: SAHD (Sick As Hell Disorder).

Between the two of us, we should manage to get this patient pregnant.

The patient was to have a bowel resection but took a job as a banker instead.

The rectal examination indicated no malfunction of the thyroid gland.

GRAPHIC GRAFFITI

For a message from your Premier, press here.

> *Above the button on a hot-air*
> *hand drier in a men's washroom,*
> *Prince George, British Columbia*

I'm so horny, even the crack of dawn won't be safe tomorrow.

> *On the wall of a men's washroom stall, Winnipeg,*
> *Manitoba*

The fire brigade is looking for new recruits. If you can reach this mark, we'd like to hear from you.

> *High on the wall of a urinal,*
> *Villa Park, Illinois*

Watch out for small, thin limbo dancers.

> *On bottom of stall door, women's restroom, Seattle,*
> *Washington*

For self-portrait, pull and wipe.

> *Above the toilet paper dispenser in a men's wash-*
> *room, Victoria, British Columbia*

Flush three times—100 yards to the cafeteria.

> *Above toilet, men's washroom,*
> *Portland, Oregon*

Do NOT eat the big white mint!

> *Above urinals in Country and Western bars across*
> *the south.*

EYE SEES

Two friends were walking their dogs. One had a Doberman Pinscher and the other a Chihuahua. After a few minutes, they got thirsty and the one with the Doberman suggested they go for a drink.

"They'll never let us into the bar with these dogs," his friend replied.

"You're wrong about that," answered the Doberman walker, "Just put these dark glasses on and follow my lead."

They crossed the street and entered a bar. Immediately, a bouncer came over and told them to leave. The Doberman walker replied, "You can't do that. It's against the law. I'm legally blind and this is my seeing-eye dog."

The bouncer backed off and let him sit down and order a drink. But he blocked the way of the Chihuahua owner.

"Sorry buddy. You can't drink here with that pet," said the bouncer.

"Oh," replied the Chihuahua walker, "I'm legally blind. This is my seeing-eye dog."

"Don't give me that," said the bouncer. "A Chihuahua, a damn Chihuahua?"

The guy with the small dog then shouted, "You mean I've been risking my life with a Chihuahua! Can you believe that, they assigned me a Chihuahua!"

RELIGIOUS CONVERSION

A church and a synagogue were situated on opposite sides of the street. The priest and the rabbi from these establishments were good friends and, because their schedules were so very similar, they decided to buy a jointly-owned automobile. After purchasing this new car, they drove it back and parked it in the street midway between the two buildings. Half an hour later, the rabbi happened to look out of the synagogue and noticed that the priest was sprinkling water all over the car. He couldn't understand this because the car was new, clean and certainly didn't need washing. He ran out and asked the priest what he was doing.

"Well," came the answer, "we don't want any breakdowns, or payment problems, so I'm blessing it with Holy Water."

The rabbi thought for a moment, went back into the synagogue and returned with a hacksaw. He then ran to the back of the car and cut a couple of inches off the tail pipe.

COMPARE THESE: TRUE BUT STRANGE

Abraham Lincoln was elected to Congress in 1846 and John F. Kennedy in 1946.

Lincoln became President in 1860 and Kennedy in 1960.

Both Presidents were shot in the head on a Friday.

Lincoln had a secretary called Kennedy and Kennedy had one named Lincoln.

Both were succeeded by a Johnson. Andrew Johnson, who succeeded Lincoln, was born in 1808, while Lyndon Johnson, Kennedy's successor, was born in 1908.

Lincoln's assassin, John Wilkes Booth was born in 1839 and Lee Harvey Oswald in 1939. Both were assassinated themselves before they could be tried.

A week before his assassination, Lincoln was in Monroe, Maryland, while seven days before he was shot, Kennedy was in Marilyn, Monroe.

WHAT DO THEY REALLY THINK?

The Sunday Times, London, described the results of a survey, designed to find out what women thought were the ten most attractive male physical attributes. The first of them were buttocks (actually referred to as buns by women), identified by 39% of the respondents. Then, in descending order came slimness (15%), flat stomach (13%), eyes (11%), long legs (6%), and tallness (5%). Also mentioned were hair (5%), neck (3%), penis (2%), and last and strangely least, muscular chest and shoulders (1%). That should give those body builders something to think about!

BAD NEWS FOR WOMEN DRIVERS

Stud tires out.

LONG TO BE THERE

Aischbedellazouchecastleabbe

> *Title of song (Ash forest by the bridge next to the Castle Abbe)*

Artiformologicalintactitudinarianisminist

> *One who studies 4-5 letter Latin prefixes and suffixes*

Humahumanukanukaapua'a

> *The state fish of Hawaii (Reef Trigger Fish)*

Kardivilliwarrakurrakurrieapparlandoo

> *Name of a lake in Northern Australia*

MOTHER'S DAY

Soon after her son's birthday, a mother was knitting in the living room, listening to him play with his new train set in the dining room. The train stopped, and she heard the following announcement, "Every son of a bitch that wants to get off, get the hell out of here now, because this is our last stop. All you sons of bitches that are getting on, move your asses because we are behind schedule and want to leave right now."

The mother was horrified and rushed into the dining room.

"Stop that this minute. Bad language like that isn't acceptable in this house! Now go up to your room, think about what you have just said and, when you come down again in three hours, I want you to use much nicer language when you play."

Three hours later, the boy appeared and started the train again. It soon stopped at a station and the child said, "Attention, please. Those of you who are disembarking here should check the overhead rack and be sure to take all your luggage with you. We thank you for giving us the chance to serve you and we hope your journey has been a pleasant one. We would like to think that you will ride with us again soon. For those of you who are just in the process of boarding, please store your luggage in the overhead rack. You are reminded this is a no smoking train. Dinner will be served in fifteen minutes in the dining car. We will try to ensure that you have a comfortable, relaxed trip. For those of you who were totally pissed off about the three hour delay, take your complaints to the bitch in the living room."

QUESTIONABLE JOKE

An engineer and stockbroker are sitting next to one another on the long flight from San Francisco to London. The stockbroker asks the engineer if he would like to play a game, but the latter doesn't want to be bothered. He declines, pulls down the shades and tries to get a little sleep.

The stockbroker will have none of it and persists that the game is easy to play and a lot of fun. "I ask you a question and if you can't answer it, you give me $10. If you can, I give you $10. Then it's your turn to ask me a question."

The engineer explains again that he's not interested but the stockbroker is very insistent and getting rather agitated, increases the stakes.

"Okay, then," he says. "If you can't answer my question give me $10, but if I can't answer yours, you get $100 from me."

This catches the engineer's attention, so he agrees to play. The stockbroker's first question is, "Exactly how large was the national debt at noon today?"

The engineer immediately reaches into his wallet and, without saying anything, hands the stockbroker a $10 bill.

"Okay, thanks," says the stockbroker, "Now it's your turn."

The engineer then asks the stockbroker, "What is red, white, and blue and has three legs in the morning and only two in the evening?"

The stockbroker looks amazed, thinks for a while, taps into the Internet, searches numerous library archives, sends email to his co-workers and, two hours later, is ready to admit defeat. He wakes up the engineer and hands him a $100 bill. The engineer nods, takes the money and turns over to go back to sleep. The stockbroker, a little hot under the collar, shakes him and demands, "What's the answer then?"

The engineer takes out his wallet, removes $10 and gives it to the stockbroker and goes back to sleep.

TRUE LOVE

Give me my Romeo; and, when he shall die,
Take him and cut him out in little stars,
And he will make the face of heaven so fine,
That all the world will be in love with the night,
And pay no worship to the garish sun.

> *William Shakespeare*
> *"Romeo and Juliet"*

BAD RACING JOKE

Alex Anderson was watching the Kentucky Derby at
Churchill Downs. There was only one empty seat in
the stands next to Anderson. His neighbor, curious
about the vacancy, asked, "Who does that seat
belong to?"

"It's my wife's," Anderson answered.

"So where is she?"

"She died."

"Why didn't you give the ticket to one of your
friends?"

"They're all at her funeral."

THE WORLD AT LARGE

If the earth's population were shrunk proportionally down to a village of only
100 people, it would be like this:

57 Asians,

21 Europeans,

14 from the Western Hemisphere (North and South),

and 8 Africans.

Of these, 51 would be female and 49 male;

70 non-white and 30 white,

70 non-Christians and 30 Christians.

50 percent of the entire wealth would be under the control of six of the villagers,
all representing the USA.

80 would be in poor quality housing,

70 would be illiterate,

50 would be malnourished.

One would be dying and one near birth.

Only one would have been to college.

It is clear from this compressed perspective that we need tolerance and
understanding if we are to live in peace.

APPLICATION FORM-101A
PERMISSION TO DATE MY DAUGHTER

Instructions:
No dates until this form is completed. It must be accompanied by a letter of credit, a financial statement, a job listing and an up-to-date medical report. Polygraph and psychological testing may be required later.

Name: _____

Birthdate: _____ Social Security Number:_____

Driver's License Number:_____

Address: _____ Telephone:_____

Are your parents married?_____

Are your parents of opposite sex?_____

Do you own a car with a back seat?   _____

Do you have very long hair or very short hair?_____

Is your hair green/yellow/red/blue/pink/purple?_____

Do you wear an earring?_____

Do you wear two earrings?_____

Do you wear lipstick?_____

Do you have a tattoo?_____

Do you wear a belly button ring and/or a nose ring?_____

Define the following terms in 50 words or less:
LATE: _____

VERY LATE: _____

NO: _____

DON'T STOP NOW: _____

BEHAVE YOURSELF: _____

What church do you attend?_____

When is the best time to call your minister? _____

When is the best time to call your teacher? _____

When is the best time to call your parents? _____

Have you ever had your fingerprints taken? _____

Complete the following:
A woman's place is in the_____

The thing that I noticed first about your daughter was her _____

My intentions are entirely_____

I broke up with my last girlfriend because _____

DON'T CALL US, WE'LL CALL YOU.

FOOTBALL JOKE

A New York Times reporter is eating his lunch in Central Park, watching a couple of young guys passing a football. Suddenly, a very ferocious pit bull attacks one, knocking him to the ground and biting him viciously. The other guy runs over to the nearby picket fence, grabs a plank, pulls it off, and runs over to where the dog is savaging his friend. He then beats it to a pulp, so saving his comrade's life.

The reporter, sensing a story, runs over and shouts, "That's terrific, this will be on tomorrow's front page. I can see it now, GIANTS FAN PROTECTS FRIEND FROM MAN-EATER"

The young hero replies, "Well, I'm not a Giant's fan."

To which the reporter responds, "BILLS FAN PROTECTS...."

Again, the young guy shakes his head, "I don't support the Bills either, my team is the San Francisco 49ers."

The reporter responds, "The 49ers?"

"Yes, the 49ers," the young man answers.

The story is reported the next day in the New York Times. On the front page, it reads, "BELOVED FAMILY PET KILLED BY VISITING REDNECK PUNK."

TRUE WORDS FROM THE WISE

A lie can travel halfway around the world while the truth is putting on its shoes.
Mark Twain

Any fool can tell the truth, but it requires a person of some sense to know how to lie well.
Anon

Sin has many tools, but a lie is the handle which fits them all.
Anon

My way of joking is to tell the truth; it's the funniest joke in the world.
Anon

Liar: One who tells an unpleasant truth.
Anon

Please don't lie to me, unless you're absolutely sure I'll never find out the truth.
Ashleigh Brilliant

The opposite of a correct statement is a false statement. But the opposite of a profound truth may well be another profound truth.

Niels Bohr

I never give them hell. I just tell the truth and they think it's hell.

Harry Truman

Telling the truth to people who misunderstand you is generally promoting a falsehood, isn't it?

Anon

The most incomprehensible thing about the world is that it is comprehensible.

Albert Einstein

The chess board is the world, the pieces are the phenomena of the universe, the rules of the game are what we call the laws of Nature. The player on the other side is hidden from us. We know that his play is always fair, just and patient. But we also know, to our cost, that he never overlooks a mistake, or makes the smallest allowance for ignorance.

Thomas Henry Huxley

When we try to pick out anything by itself, we find it hitched to everything else in the universe.

John Muir

When you look into the abyss, the abyss also looks into you.

Friedrich Nietzche

I do not know whether I was then a man dreaming I was a butterfly, or whether I am now a butterfly dreaming I am a man.

Chang-tzu

The universe is laughing behind your back.

Anon

Natural laws have no pity.

Anon

Three may keep a secret, if two are dead.

Benjamin Franklin

Self-sacrifice enables us to sacrifice other people without blushing.

George Bernard Shaw

There comes a time in the affairs of man when he must take the bull by the tail and face the situation.

W.C. Fields

RACING AHEAD: HOW SWEET IT IS

A trainer is in the paddock tending to one of his horses, just before a big race. When he thinks nobody is watching, he puts his hand into his pocket, takes out two white cubes and feeds them to the horse. Unfortunately for him, the paddock judge turns around just as the horse is taking these treats from the trainer's hand. The judge rushes over and begins to berate him.

"You know that's illegal. Nothing can be given to a horse after testing. Now I'm going to have to disqualify him."

The trainer replies, "Be reasonable judge, it was just a couple of sugar lumps. He loves sugar and it makes him less nervous and easier to get into the starting gate. Look, here's another one. Eat it yourself."

The judge takes the cube, crushes it between his teeth and swallows.

"Alright," he says, "But this is the last warning you'll get. If it happens again, he'll be disqualified instantly."

Having given this lecture, the judge leaves, being quickly replaced by the jockey who is going to be riding the horse. The trainer starts giving him his instructions.

"Today, he'll go like the wind. Hold him back till you hit the home-stretch, then let him go. Nothing will catch him. If you hear something gaining on you, don't worry. It'll just be the paddock judge."

SHALL I REPEAT THAT?

The intelligence of the masses is small, their forgetfulness is great. They must be told the same thing a thousand times.

Adolf Hitler

KEY SCIENTIFIC QUESTION

Is there a Ring of Debris around Uranus?

WHO SAID THAT?

He missed a wonderful chance to hold his tongue.

Fate tried to conceal him by calling him Smith.

Some men are discovered; others are eventually found out.

Modesty: the subtle art of enhancing your charms by pretending to be unaware of them.

Admiration is what occurs when we notice another's resemblance to ourselves.

I am completely confident of your indiscretion.

It's a useless but absolutely essential precaution.

Forgetfulness is a gift God bestowed on debtors to compensate for their lack of conscience.

Charity begins, and usually remains, at home.

A QUESTION OF DEFINITION

President Clinton was addressing a group of elementary students, trying to get them to understand the meaning of the word disaster. To stimulate their interest, he asked for a definition of the term. Several hands were raised. He selected a little blonde girl in the front row. The girl answered, "A little boy went fishing and fell into the lake and drowned, that would be a disaster."

"Good try," said the President, "but that would be an unfortunate accident."

The hands shot up again and he picked a little red headed boy at the back.

"Well, if the school bus caught fire and all the children were killed, that would be a disaster."

"Good try," said the President, "but that would be a tragedy."

Again, hands were held high in the air and the President selected a little black girl.

"If you and Mrs. Clinton were flying back to the Whitehouse and Air Force 1 was blown up by a bomb and it crashed without any survivors, that would be a disaster," she said.

"You're absolutely right," cried the President, "Can you explain to the class why that would be a disaster?"

"Well," the little girl said, "It couldn't have been an accident and it certainly wouldn't be a tragedy."

I LIKE THAT

Today is tomorrow's yesterday, make it count.

Anon

Every person's life is a fairy tale, written by God's fingers.

Hans Christian Andersen

Most people are other people. Their thoughts are someone else's opinions, their lives a mimicry, their passions are quotations.

Oscar Wilde

Translation of a sign in a Japanese Hotel:

Guests are encouraged to take every advantage of our chambermaids.

Trying to define yourself is like trying to bite your own teeth.

Alan Wilson Watts

MOVIES YOU MUST SEE

Citizen Kane

The Princess Bride

Fearless

City Lights (Chaplin)

The Professional

Unbearable Lightness of Being

The Last of the Mohicans

Annie Hall

Rainman

The Commitments

Circle of Friends

The Star Wars Trilogy (of course)

The Warriors

Gone With the Wind

9 1/2 Weeks

Flashdance

Casablanca

After Hours (Martin Scorcese)

French Kiss

West Side Story

The English Patient (see it twice)

Rumble in the Bronx (Jackie Chan)

The Exorcist

Born on the Fourth of July

Dr. Giggles (just kidding)

Naughty Nymphs (just kidding, again)

Never see a Chevy Chase movie if you can help it . . .

BUMPER STICKERS

Just say no to sex with pro-lifers.

Why go elsewhere to be cheated? Come here first!

HELP WANTED

High Steeple Church,
178 Calvary Way,
St. Paul, Minnesota 55103
August 11, 1996

Mr. David Johnson
17 Bean Street
Winnipeg, Manitoba
CANADA M6H 4P3

Dear David,

I feel I may call you that, although we have yet to meet. Every November, I tour North America giving sermons on the evils of gambling, strong drink, smoking and sexual excess. George, a young man of about twenty-five, has accompanied me on the last four of these crusades. Unfortunately, George never accepted my message and always participated to the fullest in those activities I have just listed. As a consequence, he became a mindless, slobbering idiot, who did little more than fart, pick his nose and make rude gestures to the ladies in the audience. However, despite, or perhaps because of these activities, I found his presence on stage provided strong support for my message of abstinence.

Unfortunately, as a direct result of his lifestyle, George died in July. I am writing this letter, therefore, to enquire whether you or your brother Winston would be interested in taking his place on the crusade. The position should not prove too onerous for you since it involves little more than sitting down, passing gas and making obscene comments, talents your colleagues at the office assure me you have mastered completely and use on a daily basis.

Please think seriously about my offer and let me know, as soon as possible, if you or Winston will be able to participate in the November crusade. There will be a small stipend available, should you decide to join us and serve the Lord in this mysterious way.

Kindest regards,

Rev. Ivar Gotu, M.A., A.I.H.

A WORD FROM THE WISE

All nature is but art unknown to thee;
All chance direction, which thou canst not see;
All discord harmony not understood;
All partial evil,universal good:
And spite of pride, in erring reason's spite,
One truth is clear, whatever is, is right.

Alexander Pope

SPIT IT OUT

Who was the greatest stage performer of all time? My vote goes to Hadji Ali, known to one and all as the Amazing Regurgitator. Wildly popular at the turn of the century, Hadji Ali drew rich and poor to Vaudeville to watch his amazing act. This consisted of swallowing a wide range of unlikely objects, coins, watermelon seeds, peach pits, imitation jewelry and the like and then regurgitating them in the order his audience had demanded. But it was his finale that set him apart and above his peers. An assistant would first set up a tiny castle. Ali would then drink a gallon of water, followed by a pint of kerosene. As the drums rolled, he first ejected the kerosene, in a 6 foot arc across the stage, igniting the castle. As flames shot into the air, he would spew forth the gallon of water, extinguishing the fire and saving the castle. Now, what did you eat today?

STRANGE, STUPID, BUT TRUE

Desperate to find out the gender of their unborn child, parents-to-be are turning to the Liquid Brano test. This weird ritual, discovered by Brano's manufacturer, the Brackett Company, involves mixing this drain cleaner with an equal amount of the pregnant woman's urine. Best conducted during the sixth month of pregnancy, this test's results are interpreted from the mixture's color. Once the concoction has finished fizzing, a green color in the resultant liquid is thought to indicate a boy, while yellow is indicative of a girl. Experts say the test is correct approximately 50% of the time.

TRAVELLING IN SMALL, SOFT CIRCLES

A helicopter was lost in the fog above Seattle, with all its electronic communications and navigation equipment disabled by an electrical malfunction. The pilot was having great difficulty finding his way to the airport when, in the fog, he saw a tall building. He flew towards it, then circled around, while his co-pilot drew a crude sign in large letters which read "WHERE ARE WE?" Workers in the building, realizing the aircraft's plight, drew a large sign of their own which read "YOU ARE INSIDE A HELICOPTER." The pilot read the sign, looked at his chart and quickly steered his way to Seatac Airport. Once they had landed safely, the co-pilot asked him, "How could you navigate correctly on the strength of a dumb sign like that?"

The pilot laughed and replied, "There's only one company that provides help-lines on all its software that are technically correct but also completely useless."

THINK AGAIN

If one morning I walked on top of the water across the Potomac River, the headline that afternoon would read: PRESIDENT CAN'T SWIM.

Lyndon Baines Johnson

There was a young girl from Peru
Whose limericks stopped at line two.

Anon

It is necessary for me to establish a winner image. Therefore, I have to beat somebody.

Richard M. Nixon

Art is the unceasing effort to compete with the beauty of flowers—and never succeeding.

Marc Chagall

As a well-spent day brings happy sleep, so a life well spent brings happy death.

Leonardo Da Vinci

Surely the gods from the beginning have not revealed all to mortals, but by long seeking mortals can make progress in discovery.

Xenophanes of Colopnons

I am returning this otherwise good typing paper to you because someone printed gibberish all over it and then had the audacity to put your name on the top.

English Professor, Ohio University

SLEEP ON THESE

If you haven't missed a flight you've spent too much time in the airport.

Anon

Sleeping is no mean art. For its sake one must stay awake all day.

Friedrich Neitzsche

I learned this, at least, by my experiment: that if one advances confidently in the direction of his dreams, and endeavors to live the life which he has imagined, he will meet with a success unexpected in common hours.

Thoreau

Success is a journey, not a destination.

Anon

A friend is a present you give to yourself.

Robert Louis Stevenson

GARY'S HOLODECK

My Ten Favorite People From History To Have Shared A Bottle Of Bourbon With. Listed below in no particular order.

1. Jahinger Khan—Greatest squash player who ever lived. I have had dinner with him once but his religion prohibits him from drinking, so I'd like to see him get wasted.

2. Abraham Lincoln—my favorite president. Under the influence of alcohol, he probably gets even more prophetic and philosophical.

3. Patricia Ford—Playboy bunny, model, bimbo, etc. For obvious reasons.

4. Jesus Christ—to discuss carpentry techniques.

5. Charles Bukowski—Could he be the greatest drinker of all time?

6. Cleopatra—Large nose, but what a great asp.

7. My dog Champ. I'd get most of the booze, and he'd still wag his tail.

8. Einstein—I bet he's not so smart after a couple of shots.

9. Shakespeare—Probably take forever to figure out what he is actually saying.

10. My father.

I WISH I'D SAID THAT:
AND I WILL

Authority makes some people grow and others just swell.

Anon

What did the Maharishi Mahesh Yogi say to the New York hot dog vendor?

"Make me one . . . with everything."

Anon

Bare necessities of life: Food, clothing, and a blonde.

W.C. Fields

No law of ordinance is mightier than understanding.

Plato

To be a star, you must follow your own light,
Follow your own path,
and never fear the darkness,
For that is when the stars shine the brightest.

Anon

Passion governs, and she never governs wisely.

Anon

I'm not indecisive. Am I indecisive?

*Mayor of
St. Paul, Minnesota*

Happiness lies, first of all, in health.

George William Curtis

All adverse and depressing influences can be overcome, not by fighting, but by rising above them.

Charles Caleb Colton

May I always be the kind of person my dog thinks I am.

Anon

NO MISTAKE ABOUT IT

(Wednesday) FOR SALE: T. L. Brown has a sewing machine for sale.
Phone 427-6419 and ask to speak to Mrs. Jones who lives with him very cheap.

(Thursday) NOTICE: We regret having made a typographical error in
T.L. Brown's advertisement yesterday. It should have said:

> FOR SALE: One sewing machine available, call 427-6419 cheap Mrs.
> Jones who lives with him after 6 PM.

(Friday) NOTICE: We apologize to Mr. T.L. Brown for the errors in his
classified advertisement and for the many annoying telephone calls that he
received as a result. His advertisement should have read:

> FOR SALE: One sewing machine. Cheap. Phone 427-6419 pm and
> ask to speak to Mrs. Jones who loves with him.

(Saturday) NOTICE: I, T.L. Brown, do not have a sewing machine. I threw it in
the garbage. Do not call 427-6419 at any time for Mrs. Jones or anybody else,
this number has been disconnected. Mrs. Jones and I have not been having an
affair. She was my housekeeper until yesterday, when she quit.

YOU'D RATHER NOT HEAR THIS
UNDER THE ANESTHETIC

Save that piece. We'll want it for the autopsy.

Call the janitor, we'll be needing a mop.

Come back with that, Winston! Bad dog!

Well, if it's not his spleen or his kidney, then what the heck is it?

Hurry up! The ball game starts in 45 minutes.

Damn. Can you see my watch in there?

I thought you said 45cc's every 10 minutes, not 10cc's every 45 minutes.

Stand aside! I've dropped my contact lens.

Stop that thing beating, the rhythm's giving me a headache.

This patient has already had children, hasn't he? So what's the big deal?

Nice to see you again, Dr. Kervorkian. Want to assist?

VIRTUAL REALITY

Perception is 9/10ths of reality.

Anon

Another beautiful theory slain by an ugly fact.

Wendell Holmes

Accept the challenges of life so that you may feel the exhilaration of victory.

Anon

If you ever find happiness by hunting for it, you will find it as the old woman did her lost spectacles-on her own nose all the time.

Josh Billings

Grief can take care of itself, but to get the full value of a joy you must have somebody to divide it with.

Mark Twain

HOLY ICE

A man tells his wife he's going ice fishing but goes to the bar instead. After getting very drunk, he decides to go and catch some fish. It takes him some time to find but, eventually, he wanders out onto the ice to cut a hole.

Suddenly, a deep voice booms out of the sky, "There are no fish under that ice."

The drunk stops, looks around but sees nobody and starts his sawing again. Once again, there is a deep booming sound and a voice from the heavens declares, "As I told you already, there are no fish under that ice."

The drunk is perplexed, staggers around looking for the source of the voice but sees nobody. Finally, he picks up his saw and starts cutting the hole a third time. Just as he begins, the deep, loud voice bellows, "You have been warned three times. There are no fish."

The drunk is now completely baffled, flustered and rather scared. He looks up into the darkness and says, "Only God would know where all the fish are. Are you God?"

"No, I'm not," the voice replies. "I drive the Zamboni in this ice rink."

IDEAS AND IDEALS

The secret of managing a (baseball) club is to keep the five guys who hate you away from the five who are undecided.

Casey Stengel

I have always held firmly to the thought that each one of us can do a little to bring some portion of misery to an end.

Albert Schweitzer

I can live without money, but I cannot live without love.

Judy Garland

From the point of view of daily life and without going deeper, we exist for our fellow men, and particularly for those on whose smiles and well-being all our happiness depends.

Albert Einstein

It's better to stand on the wrong side of the ball and hit it right, than to stand on the right side and hit it wrong.

Official Motto of the National Association of Left Handed Golfers

There's none so blind as they that won't see.

Jonathan Swift

Almost everything you do will be insignificant, but it is very important that you do it.

Mahatma Gandhi

One sees great things from the valley; only small things from the peak.

G.K. Chesterton

We are each of us angels with only one wing, and we can only fly embracing each other.

Liciano De Crescenzo

Absence is to love what wind is to fire; it extinguishes the small, it enkindles the great.

Comte de Bussy-Rabnutin

A thing worth having is worth cheating for . . .

W.C. Fields

Everything in life depends on how that life accepts its limits.

Baldwin

Determine never to be idle. No person will have occasion to complain of the want of time who never loses any. It is wonderful how much may be done if we are always doing.

Anon

Our necessities are few but our wants are endless.

Anon

If you cannot lift the load off another's back, do not walk away. Try to lighten it.

Tyger

Life is wonderful without a script.

Anon

And ye shall know the truth and the truth shall make you free.

John 8:32

Fortune Cookie madness:
Confucius say: Show-off always shown up in showdown.

NEED A WORKOUT: TEN SUGGESTIONS

Activities	Calories consumed per hour
Making up your mind	200
Making up somebody else's mind	300
Running around in circles	450
Pushing your luck again	380
Building mountains out of molehills	185
Jumping to premature conclusions	520
Dragging your feet	185
Tooting your own horn	410
Letting it all hang out	325
Flying off the handle	425

REALITY REFUSES TO BE HOTWIRED

You never expected justice from a company, did you? They have neither a soul to lose, nor a body to kick.
Sydney Smith

It is only one step from the sublime to the ridiculous.
Napoleon, Emperor of France of his retreat from Moscow

Publishing a volume of verse is like dropping a rose petal down the Grand Canyon and waiting for the echo.
Don Marquis

None so deaf as those who won't hear.
16th-century English proverb

He never wrote a letter or a message wherein he did not speak of God as if the Creator was waiting to see him in the lobby.
Elbert Hubbard of Kaiser Wilhelm II

I have never seen a situation so dismal that a policeman couldn't make it worse.
Brendan Behan

A fanatic is one who can't change his mind and won't change the subject.
Winston Churchill

In Greece wise men speak and fools decide.
Anacharsis

You can't depend on your judgement when your imagination is out of focus.
John F. Kennedy

Only he can command who has the courage and initiative to disobey.
William McDougall

The best liar is he who makes the smallest amount of lying go the longest way.
Samuel Butler

The mission of the modern newspaper is to comfort the afflicted and afflict the comfortable.
Anon

I could never make out what those damned dots meant.
Lord Randolph Churchill, speaking of decimal points

Advertising is the rattling of a stick inside a swill bucket.
George Orwell

ARE YOU AT THE END OF YOUR TETHER?

July 19, 1997

Mr. Lazlo Daniels
Allcity Life Insurance,
83 Elgin Street,
Buffalo, New York
14207

Dear Mr. Daniels,

I am dictating a reply to your letter of July 2nd, in which you requested additional details of the accident leading to my recent injuries. I am a bricklayer who, until the time of my hospitalization, was working on the construction of the Milton Building in downtown Los Angeles. On Thursday, June 8th, at 5 pm, just as I was finishing work, I discovered there were some 450 pounds of bricks on the roof, that would not be needed to complete the job. Since it was growing late and my fellow workers had left, I did not want to take the time to carry the bricks down by hand but rather, I decided to lower them in a barrel. Fortunately, a pulley was attached to the side of the building on the 7th floor. I took a rope, went down to the ground, and secured one end. The other I placed around the pulley and then tied it to a barrel, which I then proceeded to fill with the surplus bricks. Once the barrel was full, I returned to the ground and untied the rope, holding it tightly to make sure the bricks came down slowly. Unfortunately, I only weigh 155 pounds and the bricks lifted me off the ground. I was so surprised, I hung on, forgetting to let go. As a result, I shot up the side of the building until, at the third floor, I met the barrel on its way down. As far as I can recall, that's how I fractured my skull. This contact only slowed me for a moment and I did not stop ascending until my right arm was deeply enmeshed in the pulley. This explains the four broken fingers and the dislocated wrist. Not wanting to fall seven floors, I still managed to hang on to the rope. However, moments later, the barrel struck the ground and its bottom disintegrated, spilling out the bricks. Since I now weighed considerably more than the barrel, I began to fall rapidly. In the vicinity of the third floor, I met the barrel on its way up. As far as I can recall, that accounts for the two fractured ankles and numerous broken toes. The contact with the barrel slowed my fall a little, which was fortunate because I soon landed on the pile of bricks, cracking five vertebrae. The pain was so intense, however, that I made the mistake of letting go of the end of the rope. Unfortunately, the barrel was now seven stories immediately above me . . .

WELCOME WISE WORDS

But beauty seen is never lost.
God's colors are fast;
The glory of this sunset heaven
into my soul has passed.
John Greenleaf Whittier

Most of the shadows of life are caused by standing in our own sunshine.
R. W. Emerson

I am an old man and I have known a great many troubles, but most of them have never happened.
Mark Twain

If you don't stand for something, you'll fall for anything.
Anon

People don't care how much you know, until they know how much you care.
Anon

If there's a hill to climb, don't think waiting will make it any easier.
Anon

Youth is a wonderful thing; it's a shame that it is wasted on children.
Anon

Do all the good you can,
By all the means you can,
In all the ways you can,
In all the places you can,
At all the times you can,
As long as you can.
John Wesley

BUMPER STINKERS

I'm changing lanes. Cover me.

I didn't fight my way to the top of the food chain to become a vegetarian.

They ARE out to get YOU.

Keep up your honking. I'm reloading.

SENSITIVITY 101

This semester the female faculty again are offering courses open to all men. Class size will be limited to 10, because course material will be challenging. Register early, demand will be high. There will be 20 lectures and associated laboratory work. These will focus on the following areas:

1. Recognizing and combating stupidity.

2. Housework for beginners.

3. P.M.S. (Please keep your Mouth Shut).

4. Separating coloreds from whites (no, not in South Africa, when doing laundry).

5. Parenting: responsibilities after conception.

6. Beyond bacon, eggs and beans— learning how to cook.

7. Understanding the Female Reaction to Male 3 AM. Drunkenness.

8. The weaker sex—you.

9. One hundred reasons why you should give flowers.

10. Garbage—what it is and where it should go.

11. Staying awake after the orgasm.

12. Gravity, physics, and the toilet seat—what goes up should come down.

13. Asking for directions when lost.

14. Being more mature than your children.

15. The art of changing underwear.

16. The channel changer does not belong to you.

17. Keeping your hair on.

18. No you don't look like Fabio, especially in the nude.

19. Keeping your eyes on the woman you're with.

20. Financial irresponsibility admitted. 5-1 is not better than 4.5 percent interest.

THOUGHTS FOR TODAY

Man errs as long as he strives.

> *Anon*

Everything has been thought of before, but the problem is to think of it again.

> *Goethe*

It ever has been since time began,
  And ever will be, till time lose breath,
That love is a mood-no more-to a man,
  And love to a woman is life or death.

> *Ella Wheeler Wilcox*

Live in conformity with nature; i.e., live naturally! (naturae convenienter vive).

> *Cicero*

Pain is inevitable, suffering optional.

> *Anon*

The reason that there are twenty million or so male sperm for each female egg is because males refuse to ask for directions.

> *after Hugh Arscott*

It's better to have loved and lost than to have loved and caught something.

> *Anon*

There are two ways to meet life; you may refuse to care until indifference becomes a habit, a defensive armor, and you are safe—but bored, or you can care greatly, and live greatly—'till life breaks you on its wheel.

> *Dorothy Canfield Fisher*

IN THE DEPTHS

I believe in the sun
even when it is not shining
I believe in love
even when I feel it not

I believe in God
Even when He is silent.

written on the wall of a concentration camp

ONE GASTRONOMIC EVENING

taken from Gary Tooze's QotD July 96:

Hiya all, I had quite an evening. I ate a 9 course meal cooked by the Epicurean Chefs Society Team that is heading to Limerick, Ireland to represent Canada in the World Championships. There were 16 chefs for 100 people and my taste buds are still spinning.

My meal:

1. Selection of Canapes
   with Rossana Banc de Blanc Methode Champenoise

2. Charred Portobello Mushrooms in white truffle ice wine essence with Gamay barrel smoked pork tenderloin and sweet pepper oil
   with 1994 Riesling Dry

3. Iced Yellow Tomato Gazpacho with chives and horseradish beetroot mousseline

4. Rainbow Trout baked in parchment envelope with chervil, lemon balm and Chardonnay butter

5. Magnotta Golden Sherry Citrus Saffron Sorbet

6. Pintelle Guinea Hen Breast with brandied sour cherries and lentils in natural pan jus
   with 1994 Gamay Noir

7. Tartlette of Ermire Cheese on Niagara rhubarb comfit
   with 1994 Late Harvest Vidal

8. White Chocolate Raspberry Charlotte on orange pekoe custard cream
   with 1994 Select Late Harvest Vidal

9. Petit Fours
   *with 1994 Vidal Icewine
   Limited Edition*

Think I'll stay in bed
Wednesday.
Cheers, Gary.

TOO TRUE

There are few wild beasts more to be dreaded than a communicative man having nothing to communicate.
Christian Nestell Bovee

He's right . . . if ya got nothin' important to say today . . . keep quiet!

When people are free to do as they please, they actually imitate each other.
Eric Hoffer

Man lives in only one small room of the enormous house of consciousness.
William James (paraphrased)

JESUS SAVES

The burglar was driving slowly through a high-class suburb. Outside one large house, a moving van was being unloaded and a stereo, big screen television set, silverware and antique paintings were being carried into the building. He made a mental note to return soon and drove on.

Three days later, as he was prowling the neighborhood again, he noticed an old couple outside the same house loading suitcases into the trunk of their car. He found it difficult to contain his excitement. There was a new moon and the sky was overcast, so that it was extremely dark when he returned late the same evening. As he expected, nobody answered his call when he rang the doorbell, so he went to the back of the house, broke a window and climbed in. The house inside was as dark as a grave and with the help of a flashlight, he made his way into the dining room and then the den. Just as he was about to carry a stereo to the front door, a voice said, "I see you!" and then "Jesus saves."

Immediately, he froze in his tracks.

Nothing else happened and so he shone his flashlight towards the source of the voice. All he could see was a large red and green parrot, sitting on its swing in a cage. Again it repeated, "I see you" followed by "Jesus saves."

The burglar started to laugh. "You dumb bird. Say that again and I'll ring your damn neck."

The burglar went to the window, pulled the drapes closed and turned on the lights. Sitting beneath the parrot's cage was a huge, fearsome, angry Doberman Pincher.

"Get him Jesus! Get him!" said the parrot.

THOUGHTS MORE OR LESS ANON

Heat is required to forge anything. Every great accomplishment is the story of a flaming heart.

Some people want to learn things they do not know, while others do not wish to know the things they have learned.

Attitudes are more important than facts.

Throw your heart over the bar and your body will follow.

The rough is only mental.

Winners focus on concepts of solutions rather than concepts of problems.

Winners see risks as opportunity. They see the rewards of success in advance. They do not fear the penalties of failure.

Out of DESIRE comes the energy and will to win.

Don't take counsel from your fears and don't worry about them.

Don't be a cloud just because you aren't a star.

That which you fear or expect most will surely come to pass; the body manifests what your mind harbors.

If you love yourself, then you can give love. How can you give what you don't have?

Life is a do-it-yourself project. I take the credit or the blame for my performance.

Winners dwell on their desires, not their limitations.

Doubters don't win. Winners never doubt.

The beginning is the most important part of the work.
Plato, The Republic. Book II

It is the greatest of all mistakes to do nothing because you can only do a little. Do what you can.
Sydney Smith

Our doubts are traitors, and make us lose the good we oft might win, by fearing to attempt.
William Shakespeare

After reading these, you should be ready to take on the world. Go get 'em tiger.

CAN THIS BE TRUE?

Quotation, n. The act of repeating erroneously the words of another. The words erroneously repeated.

Ambrose Gwinett Bierce The Devil's Dictionary

Poverty is the mother of crime.

Magnus Aurelius Cassiodorus

—so why do the rich still steal? Maybe greed's the father.

Mejor morir a pie que vivir en rodillas.
(Better to die on one's feet than live on one's knees.)

Delores Ibarruri Gomez

Life may at times be boring, but is it more fun to be dead?

Alcor Life Extension Foundation

Living is not breathing but doing.

Rousseau

He reminds me of the young man who was found guilty of murdering both his parents, and when the judge asked if there were any ameliorating circumstances, pleaded for mercy on the grounds that he was an orphan.

Anon

THE GIFT

Bennet Cerf relates this heart-rending short story about a drama that took place in a bus that was bouncing along a back road in the Deep South. On one seat sat on old gentleman, clutching a bunch of fresh flowers. Across the aisle was sitting a young girl, who kept eyeing his bouquet. When it was time for him to get off, the old man impulsively thrust the flowers into the girl's hands.

"It's obvious," he said, "that you love flowers and I'm sure my wife would like you to keep these."

The girl accepted them with a smile and then watched as the old man got off the bus and walked slowly through a cemetery gate.

A MATTER OF LEGAL ETHICS

A university professor, priest and lawyer were awakened by telephone in the middle of the night and asked to visit a mutual friend who was dying. All three rushed to his bedside. On arrival, they found he was still able to speak but only in a whisper. He waved them over to his bed and in a low, croaking voice said, "My relatives can hardly wait for me to die. They all expect to become wealthy at my expense, but I'm going to fool them. Under this bed are three briefcases. I have sold everything I own, including this house and all my cash is in those three cases. I have called you here because you are the only people I trust. Tonight, when you leave, please take a briefcase. In each is $500,000. At my funeral, just before they close the casket, I expect each of you to slip that money under my body. I'm going to punish my relatives by taking it with me."

The three professional men were amazed, but felt this was the least they could do for a dying friend. Each took a briefcase. Six days later, they met again at the wake, following their friend's funeral. As they were eating from the buffet provided for the event, the professor began to talk to the priest.

"Father," he said. "I feel terrible, for I have sinned."

The priest replied, "What is it my friend? You can confide in me."

"Well," answered the professor, "You see my new car parked outside. Well, it looks so good when I leave it in the driveway of my new home. To cut a long story short, I deceived a dying friend and only left $150,000 in his coffin."

"Well," said the priest, "The Lord, Himself works in mysterious ways. Did you happen to see the new roof of St. Joseph's when you drove past in your car? Or could you hear the new organ? Don't feel so bad, my own contribution to the coffin was only $120,000."

The lawyer, who had been standing close by, then broke into the conversation.

"I can't believe it," he said, "You a tenured faculty member at a well established university and you father, a priest serving the spiritual needs of thousands, both stealing most of the life savings of a dying man. Is nothing sacred? Well I want you to know, one of us kept his word. Not only did I put the full $500,000 into the coffin but I added $5000 in interest to my cheque!"

A LITTLE INSIGHT

Come madam wife, sit by my side, and let the world slip by, we shall ne'er be younger.

Shakespeare, Taming of the Shrew

IS THAT POLITIC?

I haven't committed a crime. What I did was fail to comply with the law.

New York City Mayor,
answering accusations that he failed to pay his taxes

To forgive is to set a prisoner free, and discover the prisoner was YOU.

Anon

I have learned, in whatsoever state I am, therewith to be content.

Epistle of Paul the Apostle to the Philippians 4:11

Sometimes a noble failure serves the world as faithfully as a distinguished success.

Edward Dowden

Don't talk about yourself. They will do that after you leave.

after Addison Mizner

Let feeble souls, from fear of absurd egotism, cherish such thoughts. I am satisfied with the mystery of the eternity of life and a glimpse of the marvellous structure of the existing world, together with the devoted striving to comprehend a portion, be it ever so tiny, of the reason that manifests itself in nature.

Albert Einstein

Truth is stranger than fiction because fiction has to make sense.

Mark Twain

DO YOU MIND?

The mind is its own place, and in itself can make heaven of Hell, a hell of Heaven.

Milton

The play was a great success, but the audience was a failure.

Oscar Wilde

Once a change of direction has begun, even though it's the wrong one, it tends to clothe itself as thoroughly in the appurtenances of rightness as if it had been natural all along.

Scott Fitzgerald

The reward of suffering is experience.

Aeschylus

CHEW ON THESE

No man was ever so much deceived by another as by himself.

Anon

The best bridge between hope and despair is often a good night's sleep.

Anon

The public is a fool.

Alexander Pope

Experience is the name everyone gives to their mistakes.

Oscar Wilde

Brief is the space of life allotted to you; pass it as pleasantly as you can, not grieving from noon to eve.

Euripedes

JUST A THOUGHT

If you don't expect much, you may not be let down.

after Gin Blossoms

Religion is something left over from the infancy of our intelligence, it will fade away as we adopt reason and science as our guidelines.

Bertrand Russell

In research, you must remember not to fool yourself, for you are the easiest person to fool.

Richard Phillips Feynman

Hate the sin and love the sinner.

Mahatma Gandhi

THOUGHT FOR THE DAY

The man I live with is a cheating, no good lush. Why, he's so unreliable I'm not even sure the child I'm carrying belongs to him.

MORE WISE WORDS

The older you are the better you once were.

after John McEnroe

I always turn to the sports page first. The sports page records people's accomplishments; the front page but man's failure.

Earl Warren

Education is the ability to listen to almost anything without losing your temper or your self-confidence.

Robert Frost

To be bitter is to waste precious moments of a life that is too short already.

Anon

No one is guaranteed happiness. Life just gives each person time and space. It is up to us to fill it with joy.

Anon

The people in this world are not standing single file. Look closely. Everyone is standing in a circle, holding hands. Whatever you give to the person next to you, it eventually comes back to you.

Anon

Bobby Knight told me this: 'There is nothing that a good defence cannot beat a better offence.' In other words a good offence wins.

Vice President Dan Quayle comparing the offensive capabilities of the Warsaw Pact with the defensive system of NATO

COPY THIS

In a recent survey to find out why so many paper copies were being made, the committee studying the topic decided to make duplicates for a week of everything that was being copied in major government departments. This is not surprising. Americans now make almost 400 billion photocopies each year, about 750,000 per minute. If each copier used 5 fewer copies every business day, either by reproducing on both sides of the paper or by avoiding unnecessary use, 17.5 million reams of paper would be saved. This is the equivalent of 1.4 million trees. The more sophisticated copiers have an energy saving feature. If only 10 percent of all copiers were equipped with this, or were switched off when not being used, 7 billion kilowatt hours of electricity could be saved, about the energy equivalent of 4 million barrels of oil.

WHO CARES?

It may be that the race is not always to the swift, nor the battle to the strong—but that is the way to bet.

Damon Runyan

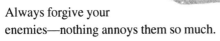

Failure isn't falling down. Failure is staying down.

Anon

Always forgive your enemies—nothing annoys them so much.

Oscar Wilde

If you're handed Lemons, make Lemonade.

Anon

ORIGINAL SIN

About six weeks ago, a Frenchman went to his local Catholic church to confess.

"Forgive me, father," he said, "for I have surely sinned. During the Second World War, I hid a Jewish jeweller in my basement."

"But my son," replied the priest, "that was not a sin. It was an act of courage, a brave act of brotherhood."

"But father," continued the man, "I sinned because I charged him 100 Francs a week to stay there."

"Well," said the priest, "that wasn't very Christian, but I suppose you had overheads. It wasn't really a sin."

"But father," said the man, "I still haven't told him the war is over."

THINK ABOUT THIS

If your cloak was a gift, I appreciate it; if it was a loan, I'm not through with it yet.

Diogenes

We have complicated every simple gift of the Gods.

Diogenes

CAN THIS ALL BE COINCIDENTAL?

Jesus is the Good Shepherd.
Elvis dated Cybill Shepard.

Jesus was part of the Trinity.
Elvis' first band was a trio.

Jesus could walk on water. (Matthew 14:25)
Elvis could surf. (Blue Hawaii, Paramount, 1965)

Jesus' Apostles numbered 12.
Elvis' entourage, the Memphis Mafia, had 12 members.

Jesus was resurrected at Easter.
Elvis had his famous 1968 "comeback" TV special.

Jesus said, "If any man thirst, let him come unto me, and drink." (John 7:37)
Elvis said, "Drinks on me!" (Jailhouse Rock, MGM, 1957)

Jesus fasted in the desert for 40 days and nights.
Elvis had irregular eating habits. He ate as many as 6 banana splits for breakfast.

Jesus was born on December 25th and, therefore, was a Capricorn.
Elvis, born January 8th, also was a Capricorn.

Jesus' countenance was like lightning, and his raiment white as snow.
    (Matthew 28:3)
Elvis often wore snow-white jumpsuits with lightning bolts.

Jesus lived in state of grace in a Near Eastern land.
Elvis lived in Graceland in a nearly eastern state.

Jesus was known as the Lamb of God.
Elvis had mutton chop sideburns.

Jesus' Father, God, is everywhere.
Elvis' father was a drifter, and moved around constantly.

Jesus said, "Man shall not live by bread alone."
Elvis liked his sandwiches to include both peanut butter
    and bananas.

There is definitely less to this than meets the eye.
    Why don't they teach this in school?
    Another conspiracy?

ATTENTION ALL ENVIRONMENTALISTS

When you die, your body will either decompose and pollute the groundwater or be cremated and diminish air quality. Does this bother you? If so, why not consider the alternative, a Tibetan sky burial? Your body will be mounted on a rock, where body breakers will hack it to pieces with knives and machetes. Your bones will then be broken into powder by mallets. Once your head has been severed, skinned and crushed, the rock will be overflowing with your flesh, blood, intestines, and brains. This human pulp finally will be mixed with tsampa (roasted barley-flour) and then the body breakers will depart. The air will soon turn black with the beating wings of hundreds of vultures, ready to begin their feeding frenzy. After you are nothing more than a memory, these birds, too full to fly, will waddle away to sleep you off.

based on a description by Michael Buckley in
Cycling to Xian and Other Stories — *great book.*

HAPPINESS OF CAUSE

	Single Men	*Single Women*	*Married Men*	*Married Women*
Friends and social life	1	1	8	8
Job or primary activities	2	3	4	7
Being in love	3	2	2	1
Recognition (success)	4	4	7	5
Sex	5	6	6	4
Personal growth	6	5	1	6
Finances	7	9	10	—
Home	8	10	—	—
Body and attractiveness	9	8	—	—
Health	10	7	—	9
Marriage	—	—	3	2
Partner's happiness	—	—	5	3
Being a parent	—	—	9	10

Based on data from Happy People New York; *Harcourt, Brace, Janovnovich.*

SOMETHING LOST IN TRANSLATION?

Office of an Italian physician: Specialist in diseases, including women.

Beijing hotel: The water and other drinks in this establishment have all been passed by the manager.

Costa Rican shop: While our nylons may cost you more, you'll find them better for the long run.

Majorcan shop door: Here we is English talking, also speeching American.

Club entrance Barcelona: Very select. Members and non-members only.

Tokyo hotel: It is forbidden to steal towels. If you are not a person to do such deeds do not read this notis, please.

Bucharest hotel lobby: Lift broken. Take care, today we are unbearable.

Paris laundry: Ladies leave your underwear here and spend the afternoon having a good time.

German Inn: Special today—no ice cream.

Singapore airline ticket office: Say goodbye to your bags here.

Hong Kong tailor's shop: Have your fits upstairs.

Paris dress shop: Ideal dresses for street walking.

Moscow hotel: Our guests are welcome to visit the cemetery where famous Russian and Soviet composers, artists and writers are buried daily, except Wednesday.

COMPOSE YOURSELF

Two American tourists took advantage of the opportunity to visit the Russian cemetery, described above and were delighted to stumble across Beethoven's grave. It was early in the morning and very quiet. As they knelt beside the grave to pay homage, they could swear they heard some very faint music. Nevertheless, they were unable to identify what was being played. The next morning, they returned with a more knowledgeable friend who immediately identified it as Beethoven's sixth symphony being played backwards. They returned the next day, only to hear the faint strains of Beethoven's fifth symphony being played in reverse. Amazed by these phenomena, they searched Moscow for a psychic and paid him to visit the cemetery with them, early the following day. At that time, Beethoven's fourth symphony was being played backwards. This, however, did not trouble the psychic who explained, "It's nothing unusual here, it's just Beethoven decomposing."

PAWS FOR CONCERN

The Top 20 Reasons My Dog "CHAMP" Doesn't Use My Computer:

20. 'Cause dogs ain't GEEKS! Now, cats, on the other hand . . .

19. Fetch command not available on all platforms.

18. Hard to read the monitor with your head cocked to one side.

17. Too difficult to "mark" every website he visits.

16. Can't help attacking the screen when he hears "You've got mail."

15. Annoyed by lack of newsgroup, alt.pictures.master's.leg

14. Involuntary tail wagging is dead giveaway he's browsing www.penthouse.com instead of working.

13. Keeps bruising nose trying to catch MPEG frisbee.

12. Not at all fooled by Chuckwagon Screen Saver.

11. Still trying to come up with an "emotion" that signifies tail-wagging.

10. Oh, but he WILL . . . as soon as he grows an Opposable Thumb.

9. Three words: Carpal Paw Syndrome.

8. Can't stick his head out of these Windows.

7. Barking in next cube keeps activating YOUR voice recognition software.

6. SmellU-SmellMe Hardware still in beta testing.

5. Does not find www.Garfield.com at all amusing.

4. Saliva-coated mouse gets mighty difficult to maneuver.

3. Fire hydrant icon simply frustrating.

2. Butt-sniffing more direct and less deceiving than online chat rooms.

and the Number 1 Reason Champ Doesn't Use My Computer . . .

1. lrwrk8794nmncdl1234;/c[rjfjkr;fo2934nf[03-fjk'1p,. *

HMMM—MAYBE

Do you recall when German Silva won the New York City Marathon, despite taking a wrong turn and considerably increasing the length of the race? Well, according to Dennis Miller, immediately after the race ended, Silva was offered a job as a Manhattan cab driver.

•••

In his 1976 book, *Media Sexploitation*, advertising guru Wilson Bryan Key claimed that the word SEX was baked onto the surface of a well known brand of crackers, scrawled in the irregular mottling of the surface. He suggested there are about a dozen SEXes, all in capitals, on both the cracker's tops and bottoms. To identify them, he suggests placing them face up and gazing at them for a few minutes. If that doesn't work, turn the lights down low, put on soft music and open the wine.

•••

No man is lonely while eating spaghetti.

Anon

DO YOU RECALL THIS?

An elderly man and his wife were both having memory loss problems. After a series of minor disasters, they went to see their doctor, to ask for his advice.

"Well," he said. "Many senior patients of mine find it extremely helpful to write themselves little notes, so that they don't forget what they are going to do."

The couple thanked him and went home, thinking this was a good idea.

The next day was her birthday and she asked her husband to get her an ice cream to celebrate.

"You'd better write that down before you go to the refrigerator," she said.

"Nonsense," he replied. "There's no way I'll forget that."

"And add raspberries," she continued, "Write that down."

"No need," he replied, "no need."

"Well," she answered. "I'd also like a cream topping. You'd better write a note about that."

"No, no," he said. "I'll easily remember an ice cream with raspberries and a cream topping."

Her husband then disappeared into the kitchen. Fifteen minutes later, he returned with a plate of bacon and eggs. She looked at it for a moment and said, "I knew you'd forget something. Where are the beans?"

I'LL DRINK TO THAT

An Irishman walks into a pub in London, orders three pints of beer and slowly sips from each one in turn. Finally, when he has emptied all three glasses, he orders three more.

The bartender says to him, "You know, after a while, a pint goes flat; they would keep their taste better if you bought just one at a time."

To which the drinker replies, "Well you see, I have two brothers, one is in Brazil and the other is in Turkey, and I'm alone here in London. When we were separating, we promised that no matter where we were, we'd each drink like this to remind us of the great times we've spent together."

The bartender admits this is an interesting custom and says nothing further about the unusual method of ordering.

The Irishman becomes a regular in the bar, and always drinks three pints at once. Then one day, he comes in and only orders two pints. This upsets the other regulars who all fall silent.

When the Irishman returns to the bar for another two glasses of beer, the bartender says, "I don't want to intrude on your grief, but on behalf of everybody here, I'd like to express my condolences on the death of your brother."

The man is confused for a moment, then a light dawns and he begins to laugh.

"No, no," he says. "Both my brothers are in good health. It's just I've joined AA and quit drinking."

THE 372 CONSPIRACY

Take an American 5 dollar bill and examine the back, especially the Lincoln Memorial. Look at the bushes to the left of the steps leading up to the Memorial. The pattern of shading appears to spell out a three digit number 372. These numerals are dark against a lighter background. The 3 has an exaggerated lower stroke; the 7 has a strong downward serif at the left end of the horizontal stroke while the shadow in the bushes on the right form no coherent pattern. Once you see the 372, it's hard not to recognize it! Can anyone tell me the significance of this number? The US Treasury Department doggedly maintains that the appearance of this number is an accident of engraving. Hmmmmm . . .

CLASSIFIED: WOMEN SEEKING MEN

Code Word	Meaning
40-ish	48.
Adventurer	Has had more partners than you ever will.
Affectionate	Possessive.
Artist	Unreliable.
Athletic	Flat chested.
Average Looking	Ugly.
Beautiful	Pathological liar.
Commitment-minded	Pick out curtains, now!
Communication important	Just try to get a word in edge-wise.
Contagious smile	Bring your penicillin.
Educated	College dropout.
Emotionally secure	Medicated.
Employed	Has part-time job stuffing envelopes at home.
Enjoys art and opera	Big snob.
Enjoys nature	Climbs for fun.
Exotic beauty	Would frighten a Martian.
Feminist	Will tell you your problems.
Financially secure	One paycheck from the street.
Free Spirit	Uses wide range of drugs.
Friendship first	Single mother, learned lesson.
Fun	Irritating.
Gentle	Frigid.
Good listener	Incapable of conversation.
Humorous	Vicious.
Intuitive	Never uses logic.
In Transition	Needs sugar-daddy to pay for previous mistakes.
Light Drinker	Attending AA.

Looks younger	Self-deceptive, bad eyesight.
Loves travel	You pay airline, hotels.
Loves animals	House full of cats, dogs, etc.
Mature	Will not let you treat her like a farm animal in bed, like last boyfriend did.
New-Age	All body hair, all the time.
Non-traditional	Witch.
Old-fashioned	Missionary position, in the dark.
Open-minded	Very desperate.
Outgoing	You'll need earplugs.
Passionate	Nymphomaniac.
Petite	Wouldn't stand out in a pack of munchkins.
Poet	Manic depressive.
Professional	Hard as a rock.
Redhead	Shops on the hair-coloring aisle.
Reliable	Frumpy.
Reubenesque	Very fat.
Romantic	Best seen by candle light.
Self-employed	Unemployable.
Smart	Will constantly put you down.
Spiritual	Cult disciple.
Stable	Boring.
Tall, thin	Anorexic or marathon runner, or both.
Tan	Wrinkled.
Voluptuous	See Reubenesque.
Wants soulmate	May stalk you.
Weight proportional to height	Hugely fat.
Widow	Nagged first husband to death.
Writer	Once published letter to the editor.
Young at heart	Old.

And now for something completely different.

CLASSIFIED: MEN SEEKING WOMEN

Code Word	*Meaning*
50-ish	61 and looking for 27 year old women.
Affectionate	Hard-up and in need of financial support.
Artistic	Tell me how much you love my work. Ego problem.
Athletic	Watches ESPN non-stop.
Average looking	Don't expect Fabio or Paul Newman, more likely Alfred E. Neuman.
Distinguished looking	Fat, bald with glasses.
Educated	Will always treat you like an idiot.
Employed	Stacks supermarket shelves.
Financially secure	Will spend money on you, but expects return on investment.
Free spirit	What does your sister do while you're out of town?
Friendship first	Just joking.
Fun	Has repertoire of boring, dirty jokes.
Good Looking	Arrogant son-of-a-bitch.
Honest	O.K. so I lie.
Huggable	If you can get your arms around me.
ISO Slim, attractive female	Would be better off with a Labrador retriever.
Light drinker	AA, twice a week.
Likes to cuddle	Insecure, overly dependent.
Mature	More grown up than your youngest child.
Open-minded	Will sleep with your mother or her friends.
Physically fit	Addicted to mirrors.
Poet	Writes on bathroom stall walls.
Professional	Owns a white button down.
Reliable	More often than not, shows up.

Self-employed	Unemployable.
Sensitive	Don't expect me to protect you.
Smart	Likes Cheers and Married With Children.
Spiritual	Baptized.
Stable	Occasional stalker, but never arrested.
Thoughtful	Will apologize after forgetting anniversaries.
Virile	Walks his dog and still makes out once a night.
Young at heart	Lock up your children; pedophile.

THAT'S LIFE

There are two natures at war in each of us, the evil and the good.
The fight between them lasts a lifetime, and one is always in command.
In our hands lies the power of choice—we are what we most want to be.
What we most want to be, we are.

Anon

The pain of stupidity is dulled by the anesthetic of egotism.

after Frank Leahy, former Notre Dame football coach

It's not my love of animals that makes me a vegetarian; it's my hatred of plants.

after A. Whitney Brown

The most important feminine trait is always that lacking in the woman you
are dating.

after Joseph Telushkin

While there are many false prophets, there are many more false disciples.

Anon

Cursed is he that does not know when to shut his mind. An open mind is all very
well in its way, but it ought not to be so open that there is no keeping anything in
or out of it. It should be capable of shutting its doors sometimes, or may be
found a little draughty.

Samuel Butler

Atta Boy, George, we miss ya: Dumb Quote of the Day:
I have opinions of my own—strong opinions—but I don't always agree with them.

George Bush

MORE FOOD FOR THOUGHT

Everything has been thought of before, but
the problem is to think of it again.

Goethe

Genius is the ability and willingness to do
hard work, and any other concept is a
doubtful, if not dangerous, proposition.

Edison

Love's wounds can be healed only by the
one who inflicts them.
(Amoris vulnus idem sanat, qui facit).

*Publilius Syrus (85
BC-43 BC)*

Great spirits have always encountered fierce opposition from mediocre minds.

Einstein

You have to go through what you did to get where you are now, so look ahead—
that's where your future lies.

Anon

If only the people who worry about their liabilities would think about the riches
that they possess, they would stop worrying. Would you sell both your eyes for a
million dollars . . . or your two legs . . . or your hands . . . or your hearing? Add
up what you have, and you'll find that you won't sell them for all the gold in the
world. The best things in life are yours, if you can appreciate yourself. That's
the way to stop worrying—and start living!

Dale Carnegie

Everything in life depends on how that life accepts its limits.

Baldwin

Frances has the most beautiful hands in the world, and someday I'm going to
make a bust of them.

Samuel Goldwyn

Sze-Kung asked him, "Is there one word which may serve as a rule of practice
for all one's life?" The Master replied, "Is not Reciprocity such a word? What
you do not want done to yourself, do not do to others.

Confucius

The secret of the magic of life consists in using action in order to attain non-action. One must not wish to leap over everything and penetrate directly.

Lu Yen

Desire and force between them are responsible for all our actions; desire causes our voluntary acts, force our involuntary.

Pascal

The deed is everything; the glory is naught.

Goethe

Logic gives a man what he needs; magic gives a man what he wants.

Anon

The more we do, the more we can do; the more busy we are, the more leisure we have.

William Hazlitt

Our acts make or mar us; we are the children of our own deeds.

Victor Hugo

We are what we repeatedly do. Excellence, then, is not an act, but a habit.

Aristotle

Life is like a good book. The further you get into it, the more it makes sense.

after Harold S. Kushner

Hospitality is making your guests feel at home, even though you wish they were.

Anon

With proper diet, rest, and exercise, a healthy body will last a lifetime.

Anon

If there is anything the nonconformist hates worse than a conformist it's another nonconformist who doesn't conform to the prevailing standards of nonconformity.

Anon

If you don't find it in the index, look very carefully through the entire catalogue.

Consumer's Guide, Sears, Roebuck and Co. (1897)

In three words I can sum up everything I have learned about life: 'it goes on'.

Robert Frost

Leaders are like eagles: they don't flock, you find them one at a time.

Anon

TENURE TROUBLE

To President A.L. Ambrose
From Dr. J. Stansfield, Chairperson, Advisory Committee on
Appointments, Reappointments, Promotion and Tenure
April 17, 1997
God's Tenure Application

The ARPT Committee has considered God's application for tenure carefully, but regretfully has reached the conclusion that it is deficient.

Specifically, God has only one major publication. Unfortunately, this was co-authored and the scale of God's involvement is questionable and difficult to establish. In addition, the volume originally was written in Hebrew and its major hypothesis has never appeared in a peer reviewed journal. Although it is true that this work has been reprinted frequently, nothing new of substance has been added to later editions. The members of the committee who have read the publication in question also point out that it does not include either a literative review, or references. The claim that God has inspired others to write appears to be irrelevant to the matter under discussion.

Serious questions also have been raised about God's ability to conduct research. To illustrate, His willingness to cooperate with colleagues is in question. While He claims to have created the Earth in six days, there were no witnesses. Beyond this, no member of the scientific community has ever been able to replicate this experiment, throwing considerable doubt on its authenticity. Even if His claim is eventually vindicated, the committee feels obliged to point out that, at no time did God apply to the Board of Ethics for permission to experiment with human subjects. Indeed, it is very unclear whether He would have been permitted, by the Board, to do so, since His record in this respect is highly suspect. To illustrate, there is evidence to show that, when one of His early experiments went awry, God attempted to cover up the fact by drowning all but a few of His more successful subjects.

His teaching, regrettably, is also open to question. Indeed, early in His career, God expelled his first two students when they gained access to knowledge He had intended to keep to Himself. Even today, His students complain that He schedules his lectures on mountain peaks and his appearances are spasmodic and unpredictable.

While some of these publication, research, and teaching deficiencies might be overlooked, taken together they indicate a colleague who is incapable of functioning effectively in any institution of higher learning, and the committee regretfully recommends that His application for tenure be denied.

COMPUTER ENEMA

Neural networks and telecommunications are combining to bring you the virtual physician. Will you ever be able to trust your doctor who says, "Look into the monitor, drop your trousers, run the mouse up and down your legs and cough"?

ANOTHER GIFT, NOT FROM THE GODS

A rather proper young man wanted to buy a birthday present for his new girlfriend and decided that, because they had not been dating for long, a pair of gloves would be ideal: romantic yet not overly personal. Accompanied to the local shopping mall by his girlfriend's sister, he bought a beautiful pair of white gloves. At the same time, the sister purchased a pair of panties for herself.

Unfortunately, as these two items were being boxed, they became mixed. The sister was given the gloves and the young man received the panties. The box containing these he had professionally wrapped. He then sent this beautiful package to his love with the following note:

"I chose these for you because I noticed that you do not wear any when we go out. Had it not been for your sister, I would have bought you longer ones, with beautiful buttons down the side, but she persuaded me to get you shorter ones, so they will be easier to get off in a hurry.

These are a very delicate shade and I was afraid they would soil too easily. The sales-lady showed me the pair she had been wearing for two weeks and they hardly had a mark on them. She tried on yours, just to let me see what they would look like and I must say, she looked really attractive in them. I only wish I could be there to help you put them on for the first time, but no doubt many other hands will come into contact with them before mine. When you take them off, don't forget to blow on them because I'm sure you'll find they're a little damp from wearing.

I can hardly wait to kiss them on Saturday night.

P.S. The latest fashion is to wear them folded down with a little fur showing."

PASSING THOUGHTS

A state which dwarfs its men, in order that they may be more docile instruments in its hands, even for beneficial purposes, will find that with small men no great thing can really be accomplished . . . .

The end of that quote for your interest is ". . . and that the perfection of machinery to which it has sacrificed everything will in the end avail nothing, for want of the vital power which, in order that the machine might work more smoothly, it has preferred to banish."

John Stuart Mill

Diplomacy is the art of saying 'nice doggy' until you find a rock.

Will Rogers

So who's in a hurry?

ROBERT BENCHLEY in response to a warning that drinking is 'slow poison'

When you find yourself overpowered, as it were, by melancholy, the best way is to go out and do something kind to somebody or other.

John Keble

Nothing can resist the human will that will stake even its existence on its stated purpose.

Benjamin Disraeli

After all, all he did was string together a lot of old, well-known quotations.

Henry Louis Mencken, about both Shakespeare and Gary Tooze

PROGRESS

Each passing hour brings our solar system forty-three thousand miles nearer to globular cluster M13 in the constellation Hercules. Yet there are still some half-wits who continue to deny there is such a thing as progress.

after Ransom K. Ferm

DON'T CALL HER, SHE'LL CALL YOU

Darlene Snow of Dallas, Texas had a very serious problem with her telephone service. This is how she solved it.

The New Rotland Plaza Motel had been assigned almost the same telephone number as Darlene. From the first day the motel opened, Darlene was inundated with calls, not intended for her. Since she had been using her telephone number for years, she felt it only fair that the motel management arrange to change its number. The management refused, claiming it was too expensive to change its stationery and advertising.

The telephone company was just as unwilling to help, saying it was not responsible for the inability of its customers to dial correct numbers. After receiving hundreds of wrong numbers, Darlene decided it was time for action.

At 7 o'clock, her telephone rang. "Could the Rotland Plaza accommodate a party of eight, flying in from Toronto, the next day?"

Darlene answered, "No problem. How many nights?"

Then Chicago checked in and later San Francisco. A secretary from Portland wanted a suite for her boss for two weeks. Darlene gave her the Empress Suite at a discount, telling the secretary a deposit wouldn't be necessary.

The next day, Darlene was busy again making reservations for six members of an electrical engineering firm from Tokyo and a large wedding reception. Then came a college prom and a veterinarian's convention for the 4th of July weekend. Booking the ballroom for a visiting televangleist's lecture and making floral arrangements for a funeral also filled much of her time. When valet parking was discussed, Darlene advised, "There's never any charge, but we encourage you to tip the drivers."

Within a few months, the Rotland Plaza Motel was a disaster area. Customers kept arriving for bar mitzvahs, weddings, funerals, and lectures only to be told that no such events had been scheduled.

Darlene had her final revenge when the local paper finally printed a front page article about the motel's notorious unreliability and its potential bankruptcy. A few day's later, an executive from a very large chain rang and said, "We're prepared to take the place off your hands for $500,000."

To which Darlene replied, "It's a deal, but only if you'll change the telephone number."

FACTS ON FILE

For every shark attack on a human (this includes one brushing up against you in shallow water) people eat 10,000,000 sharks.

Almost 1 person in 4 in the world is of Chinese origin.

The prophet Mohammed once cut off his sleeve rather than disturb a cat that was sleeping on it.

Shakespeare's vocabulary is estimated to have been 24,000 words. The average person's is around 3,000 words.

The human heart beats 100,000 times a day.

Only men can suffer from hemophilia, but only women can pass it on from one generation to the next.

BUMPER STICKERS

Is there life before death?

There's a job for you in the Marines—mine.

There are two things I like. The other is ice cream.

I'm a virgin (This is a very old sticker!)

I'm on piece work—and the piece I'm working on is Anne.

Efficiency is laziness for the intelligent.

Sex instructor—free lessons, anytime.

Conserve water—dilute it with alcohol.

Don't criticize inflation—where would your tires be without it?

Engage brain before mouth.

This car's name is Flattery—it'll get you nowhere.

I've upped my standard of living—up yours!!

Earn cash—blackmail your colleagues.

Sex appeal—please give generously.

Don't steal—the government hates the competition.

DEFINITIONS

Cramnesia: examination induced memory loss.

Charminophobia: fear of being repeatedly squeezed.

TWENTY POLITICALLY INCORRECT WAYS OF COMMENTING ON INTELLIGENCE

Has an IQ of 3, but it takes 4 to grunt.

Proof that evolution CAN occur backwards.

As smart as chicken feed.

Warning: objects visible in mirror are dumber than they appear to be.

A few bricks short of a load.

If he had another brain, it would be lonely.

If he was smarter, he'd be a half-wit.

A few clowns short of a circus.

His belt doesn't slot through every loop.

A few beers less than a six-pack.

One cherry short of a bowl full.

One taco short of a combination plate.

His cornflake box is only half-full.

A model for Artificial Stupidity.

The wheel's still spinning, but his hamster's dead.

Not enough fries for a small order.

Couldn't hit the floor if he fell over.

Fewer genes than a fruit fly.

Missing the aces from his deck of cards.

Doesn't have all his dogs on the same leash.

SHAMELESS ADVERTISING

Madame Speaker, I feel like the only mosquito in a nudist colony. I know what I ought to do, but I'm overwhelmed by all my opportunities. When you look at the architects of Bill C-39, what do you see? Several bad comedians with stage fright, the original good time girl that was had by all, a nervous breakdown masquerading as a minister and two zipships full of 120-year-old religious fanatics intent on criticizing others' lifestyles; all fitted out like entrants in a fancy dress contest nobody else wants to attend. If this is the strongest coalition the Religious Right can throw together I can only thank God I'm still an atheist. If you must have faith in something, what about luck? How else could you explain this government's re-election?

from Harold D. Foster The Ozymandias Principles, *Southdowne Press!*

BUT IN WHICH DIRECTION?

A well-known member of the town's High Society died in the bed of a prostitute. Unfortunately, because his death was so unexpected, an inquest was inevitable. The court was full for the occasion. The lady-of-the-night, dressed in a miniskirt that left little to the imagination, was the key witness. She was sworn in.

"Now," said the judge, "in your own words, my dear, tell us exactly what happened."

"Well, your Honor," explained the prostitute, "suddenly, he let out this loud groan. I thought he was coming, but actually he was going!"

MORE PROGRESS

If the automobile had followed the computer's development cycle, a luxury car would now cost $150, get 500,000 miles per gallon and blow up once a year, killing the driver and all passengers.

after Robert X. Cringely

DEEP THINKERS

Fate is not an eagle, it creeps up like a rat.

Elizabeth Bowen

Whatever else we are intended to do, we are not intended to succeed: failure is the fate allotted.

Robert Louis Stevenson

Education: the inculcation of the incomprehensible into the indifferent by the incompetent.

John Maynard Keynes

Journalism justifies its own existence by the great Darwinian principle of the survival of the vulgarest.

Oscar Wilde

One day in retrospect the years of struggle will strike you as the most beautiful.

Sigmund Freud

A QUESTION OF DEFINITION

Politics: from the Greek 'poli' meaning multiple and 'tics' meaning blood suckers.

INSULTING DUMB BLONDE JOKES

A blonde was complaining to her mother that she was sick and tired of being called dumb. Her mother suggested that she spend time studying something interesting to impress other people.

"Why don't you learn all the state capitals or something?"

The blonde sees this as a good idea and starts working on it. In two weeks time, she feels confident that she has mastered the topic.

At the next party she attends, a guy is telling dumb blonde jokes. She indignantly goes up to him and says, "I'm NOT one of those silly women. I can name every state capital!"

To this claim, he replies, "Okay, prove it. What's the capital of Ohio?"

The blonde smiles in triumph and says, "Too easy. That's O!"

• • •

A woman decides to have the interior of her house redecorated and calls a contractor for an estimate. She tells him she wants the living room walls painted light blue. He writes something down in a notebook and then opens the window and shouts "Green side up." They go into the dining room, which she says should be pale pink. He writes in his book for a moment, goes to the window and shouts "Green side up." The woman was curious, but continues to show him the rest of the house. In each room, the pattern is repeated. When the tour is finished, the lady of the house asks the contractor why, whatever color she asks for, he feels the need to cry "Green side up," out of the window. He laughs and apologizes that it is nothing to do with her, but he has a crew of blondes laying her neighbor's lawn with new sod.

• • •

Question: What's the first thing a blonde does in the morning?
Answer: Introduces herself.

Question: What does a blonde do after sex?
Answer: Opens the car door.

Question: Why are sun-roofs popular with blondes?
Answer: More leg room.

Question: How can you tell that a blonde has been using the computer?
Answer: White-out on the screen.

MEN: A CLASSIFICATION FOR WOMEN

JOE SENSITIVE — *"After I've massaged your feet, let's cuddle."*
    AKA: Mr. Nice Guy, Family Man, Darling, Soft Boiled Eggy.
    Advantages: Spoils you; irons own shirts; well-behaved; will not stray.
    Disadvantages: Wimpy; too compassionate; boring.

OLD MAN GRUMPUS — *"The world's going to Hell in a hand basket."*
    AKA: Grumpy, Sour Puss, Natterbags, Jerk.
    Advantages: Stays on the couch; very predictable.
    Disadvantages: Pain in the butt.

SCAREDY — *"I'm sorry. Whatever it was, it was my fault. I won't do it again."*
    AKA: Creampuff, Wimpy, Hey you!
    Advantages: Stutters and jumps when deliberately startled; useful scapegoat.
    Disadvantages: Surrenders too easily; you have to protect him!

MUSCLEHEAD — *"Shut yer trap, will yer, I'm trying to think."*
    AKA: Lummox; the Incredible Bulk; Dumbo; the Ox.
    Advantages: Can move a grand piano by himself; easy to fool.
    Disadvantages: Can tear you in two; sweats; won't use deodorants; eats with
                     mouth open; snores.

THE CHEATER — *"Who me? Somebody's confusing you."*
    AKA: Snake; Rat; Son of a Bitch.
    Advantages: May feel guilty; expects you to cheat.
    Disadvantages: He's using you and proving that your
                     mother was right; probably having the
                     time of his life at your expense.

THE STUD — *"Let's make love again, after breakfast."*
    AKA: The Ace of Hearts; Casanova; Sizzler.
    Advantages: Perpetually aroused.
    Disadvantages: Perpetually aroused.

DREAMER — *"Someday, I'll be rich and you'll be*
                        famous. All we need is a lucky
                        break then . . ."
    AKA: Struggling Artist; Philosopher;
                 Wind Bag.
    Advantages: Wonderful story teller.
    Disadvantages: Tomorrow never comes.

MR. RIGHT — *"While the servants clean house and the gardener mows the*
                      lawn, why don't you and I make mad, passionate love in our
                      new yacht?"
    AKA: Jim Dandy; He's Mine; Mr. Perfect.
    Advantages: You never need to pray again, your prayers have been answered.
    Disadvantages: Virtually hunted to extinction. Few remaining examples are
                     guarded jealously.

I BEG YOUR PARDON ?

A man walks into an empty bar with a briefcase. He walks up to the bar and opens his case and pulls out a tiny piano which he places on the bar.
The bartender goes over and watches as the man then pulls out of his briefcase a small piano player who sits at the piano and starts playing. The bartender is amazed and says, "That is great, you can make millions with that act, where did you get him from?" To which the man replies, "I found a Genie's bottle and he gives a wish to anyone who rubs the bottle. Be careful, his hearing is not too good."

The bartender is more than a little skeptical and says, "Oh sure," but the man insists it is true and pulls the very bottle out of his briefcase. "Here try," he says, and places it in the bartender's hands. The bartender rubs the bottle, the Genie appears and the bartender says "Give me 50,000 bucks right now." At that very instance a "POOF POOF" sound keeps repeating and ducks start appearing throughout the bar. The bartender looks puzzled at the man and says, "What's up with this?" to which the man replies, "So you think I asked for a 14 inch pianist?"

FAST FOOD DRIVE-THRU FUN

1. Drive through backwards, yelling "WHERE'S THE CAR WASH?"
2. Ask for a half-cooked, greasy burger, badly burned fries and Coke with a dead fly in it. When they say they can't give it to you, shout "WHY NOT, THAT'S WHAT I GOT HERE LAST TIME!"
3. Stand close to the speaker and yell very loudly. Try to use as many expletives as possible so as to embarrass everybody inside.
4. When they tell you how much the order will be, ask "You don't mind if I pay in yen, do you?"
5. Say "Hi, may I take your order" to the speaker.
6. Order items such as "Cheeseburger without any bun and a small order of large fries, hold the mustard." When they query the order, ask, "Is there something wrong with your hearing?"
7. Bring your old Coke cups, burger boxes, and bags back and argue loudly that they are responsible for recycling them.
8. Place your order in a garbled, make-believe language and insist that there must be something very wrong with the speaker system.
9. Walk to the speaker, place a huge order and then walk away.
10. Put a nudists' convention banner on your vehicle and drive through with a car full of fat, naked people.

ADDITIONAL POLITICAL CORRECTNESS

She does not:
GET PMS

She becomes:
HORMONALLY CHALLENGED

She does not have:
A KILLER BODY

She is:
TERMINALLY DESIGNED

She is not:
A BAD COOK

She is:
FAST FOOD COMPATIBLE

She is not:
A POOR DRIVER

She is:
AUTOMOTIVELY DISADVANTAGED

She is not:
EASY

She is:
HORIZONTALLY FRIENDLY

She does not:
HATE SPORTS

She is:
ATHLETICALLY UNINVOLVED

She does not get:
DRUNK

She is:
ACCIDENTALLY ALCOHOL OVERSERVED

You do not ask her:
TO TANGO

You request a:
PRE-COITAL RHYTHMIC EXPERIENCE

She is not:
A GOSSIP

She is a:
VERBAL INFORMATION TRANSMITTER

She is not:
HOOKED ON SOAP OPERAS

She is:
MELODRAMATICALLY POSTGRADUATED

She is not:
FRIGID

She is:
THERMALLY DISADVANTAGED

She does not:
WEAR TOO MUCH MAKE-UP

She is:
COSMETICALLY OVEREXPOSED

Her breasts will never:
SAG OR DROOP

They will:
LOSE THEIR VERTICAL HOLD

She does not:
SPEND TOO MUCH

She is:
SUSCEPTIBLE TO MARKETING PLOYS

She is not:
TOO THIN

She is:
SKELETALLY VISIBLE

DID YOU KNOW THIS? NEITHER DID I

When cats fall from tall buildings, they always land on their feet. When you drop your morning toast, it always lands on the buttered side. Therefore, it follows, if you strap buttered toast to the back of a cat and drop the two, they will hover above the ground, unable to land. This means that, with a giant array of buttered cats for support, a monorail could easily be built from New York to San Francisco.

• • •

People yawn to equalize the air pressure on their eardrums. However, when one person does this, it alters the surrounding air pressure, forcing people nearby to yawn to equalize the air pressure on their own eardrums. This is why yawning seems to be contagious.

• • •

Mountains stick up above the earth's surface. Like the arms of a figure skater, they slow the planet's rate of spin. As the wind, rain, and glaciers erode our mountains, they are lowered in height, so increasing the earth's speed of rotation. It has been estimated that in 10 million years, when even the Himalayas and the Rockies will have been eroded down to sea level, anyone left behind on the earth will be thrown off by its dangerously fast spin.

SMART IDEAS

You cannot prevent the birds of sadness from flying over your head, but you can prevent them from nesting in your hair.
Chinese proverb

A good neighbor doubles the value of a house.
German proverb

Every man is a volume, if you know how to read him.
Anon

Dress shabbily and the world will notice the dress.
Dress elegantly, and the world will notice the woman.
after Coco Chanel

The best argument against democracy is a five-minute conversation with the average voter.
Winston Churchill

What the world calls originality is only an unaccustomed way of tickling it.
George Bernard Shaw

MALE INTELLIGENCE?

A rich man who has three lovers decides it's time to marry and settle down, but can't make up his mind which one of the women to select.
He decides to test their intelligence by giving them each $10,000 and watching how they spent it.

The blonde goes to a beauty salon for a total makeover. She then buys numerous new clothes and shoes. She tells her beau, "I spent the $10,000 making myself look beautiful for you, because I love you so deeply."

The red-head goes shopping and buys new fishing equipment, golf clubs, a season ticket to watch the local NHL hockey team and a CD player. These she presents to the man on his birthday with the words, "I'm giving you these gifts, because I love you so much."

The brunette invests the $10,000 in the stock market and quickly turns it into $50,000. She returns the $10,000 to her lover and says, "The rest I'm investing for our future, because I love you so deeply."

The man thinks carefully about what each has achieved and decides to marry the one with the biggest breasts.

IT'S DARKER THAN YOU THINK OUT THERE

One day, when I was shopping in a department store, the clerk refused my purchase when she noticed that I had failed to sign the back of my new credit card. She informed me that unless the card signature matched the one on the receipt, she had to refuse the order. She then gave me my card, which I immediately signed on the back, and returned it to her. She carefully compared the new signature on the card to the one on the receipt. As luck would have it, they matched, and my order was processed.

• • •

My friend works in the operations department in the headquarters of a large insurance company. One of their employees out in the field called in and said, "I've got smoke coming out of my computer terminal. Do you have a fire at headquarters?"

MEN: ARE YOU FEELING REJECTED?

Top 10 Rejection Lines Given by Women (and what they actually mean):

10. I think of you as my brother. (You remind me of that banjo-playing geek in "Deliverance.")

9. There's a minor difference in our ages. (I don't want to make love to someone older than my dad.)

8. I'm not attracted to you in 'that' way. (You are the ugliest S.O.B. I've ever laid eyes on.)

7. My life is rather too complicated at the moment. (I don't want you spending the whole night, or else you may hear phone calls from some of the guys I'm seeing.)

6. I've got a male friend. (I prefer my tom cat.)

5. I don't date men I work with. (I wouldn't date you if we lived in the same state, much less the same building.)

4. It's not your fault, it's mine. (It's yours.)

3. I'm concentrating on my job. (Even something as boring and unfulfilling as my career is more fun than dating you.)

2. I'm celibate. (I've sworn off men like you.)

. . . And the number 1 rejection line given by women (and what it actually means):

1. Let's be friends. (I want you to stay around, but only so I can describe to you in excruciating detail all the other men I meet and have sex with. I need that male perspective thing.)

RULES OF MY THUMB

COOKING SPAGHETTI: When spaghetti is cooked, it should stick to the wall.

WINE: One ton of grapes will make 170 gallons of wine.

REALLY GOING BALD? Normal hair loss is between one hundred to two hundred hairs a day for everyone.

PREDICTING A FROST: If the temperature is below 50 degrees Fahrenheit at sunset, expect morning frost.

YOUR ADULT HEIGHT will be double your height at age three and all boys should expect to grow taller than their mothers.

REVENGE: If you want to get your own back, try spitting into the wind.

GOOD HEAVENS

Three men die and go to Heaven. St. Peter says to the first, "I have only one question to ask you before you are allowed into Heaven: Were you completely faithful to your wife?"

The man replies, "Yes, all the time we were married, I never even looked at another woman."

St. Peter answers, "That luxury car over there is yours to drive while in Heaven."

The second man is asked the same question, and replies, "I strayed, but only once. I confessed to my wife and she forgave me."

St. Peter answers, "That convertible over there is yours to use here in Heaven."

The third man is asked the same question and answers, "I have to admit, I chased every beautiful woman I met, and that was a lot of women. And I caught most of them."

St. Peter says, "Okay, but you were basically good. That ancient sedan over there is yours to use while you're in Heaven."

The three men then separate.

A couple of weeks later, the second and third men are driving along when they see the first's luxury car parked outside of a bar. They stop their cars and go inside, only to find the driver surrounded by empty bottles, face down on the bar. They try to console him and say, "What could possibly be so terrible. You're in Heaven, driving a fancy car, and everything here is wonderful!"

To which their drunken friend replies, "I saw my wife today!"

The other two answer, "That's great! So what's your problem?"

He answers, "She was riding a tricycle!"

USELESS FACTS

At its present rate of erosion, Niagara Falls will disappear completely in only 22,800 years. What will that do to the birth rate?

Last night the Detroit String Quartet played Brahms. No one was sure of the score, but Brahms certainly lost.

after Bennett Cerf

Never, ever change horses in mid-stream.

American proverb

SENSITIVITY 102

This semester the male faculty again are offering courses open to all women. Class size will be limited to 10, because course material will be challenging. Register early, demand will be high. There will be 20 lectures and associated laboratory work. These will focus on the following areas:

1. Exercise: How it prevents you getting to look like your mother.
2. Shopping: Buying only what you can afford even if it's on sale.
3. Dishwashers: Rinsing is not necessary.
4. The physics of toilet seats: Learning how to put one down.
5. Nagging: Endless repetition as a cause of male insanity.
6. Makeup: The Less is More Hypothesis.
7. Broken Fingernails: The world will not end.
8. Not asking questions you don't want answering.
9. Exiting the washroom in under 15 minutes.
10. Housework without complaints.
11. Vacations: Why 6 suitcases is too many.
12. Hair Spray: How it is destroying the ozone layer and all life on earth. Is it worth it?
13. The Remote Control: How to select sports programs.
14. Fishing: Baiting your own hook.
15. Sex: Much more than just lying there.
16. You too can hang up the telephone.
17. Shopping is not the ultimate experience.
18. Christmas does not begin in August.
19. Learning how to choose what to wear tonight in less than 3 hours.
20. Sex is not a weapon.

THE WISDOM OF OUR ANCESTORS?

The fewer the words, the better prayer.

Luther

If you don't want to work, you have to work to earn enough money so that you won't have to work.

Ogden Nash

DON'T JUMP TO PREMATURE CONCLUSIONS

Top Ten Expressions That Sound Dirty But Really Are Not:

10. Licking the spoon.

9. Picnicking with Betty White.

8. Putting the Shot.

7. Refilling your tank.

6. Tethering the blimp.

5. Ordering in Sushi.

4. Shooting hoops with the boys.

3. Frosting the pastry.

2. Shaking hands with Ben Franklin.

and the number one . . . .

1. Camping out on Mount Baldy.

SMART

The office of government is not to confer happiness, but to give men the opportunity to work out happiness for themselves.

William Ellery Channing

Life begins at forty, but so do lumbago, bad eyesight, arthritis and the habit of telling the same story three or four times to the same listeners.

Anon

Our wretched species is so made that those who walk on the well-trodden path always throw stones at those who are showing a new road.

Voltaire

A happy family is only an early Heaven.

after Bowring

An eye for any eye can make the world blind.

Muhatma Ghandi

No snowflake in an avalanche ever feels responsible. But look at the damage they do working together.

Anon

EDUCATION: THE KEYS

My father was frightened of his father, I was frightened of my father and I am damned well going to see to it that my children are frightened of me.

King George V

If you can look very interested when really you are very bored, your social and business success is assured. It won't hurt your love life either.

Anon

It's strange how few of the earth's major problems are solved by people who remember their algebra.

after Herbert V. Prochnow

(Come to think of it, these are the people who have caused most of our problems)

All children essentially are criminals.

after Denis Diderott

CAN I INTEREST YOU IN A . . . .

Nuclear hand grenade: We've never had a customer complaint.

Fire alarm snooze bar: So why not wake up slowly?

Silicon stomach and thigh implants: Stand out in a crowd?

Inflatable dart board: With free repair kit.

Salted bandages: Speak for themselves.

Can-opener-in-a-can: We will gift-can it for you, on request.

Scrabble for dyslexics: ylno fi uoy nac daer siht.

Caviar helper: Prune-based.

Most of these inventions were provided by readers of the Washington Post *when challenged to send in useless product ideas. The idiotic comments after the product description are mine.*

BRILLIANT GOLDEN OLDIES AND MORE

I either want less corruption, or more chance to participate in it.
Ashleigh Brilliant

Please don't ask me what the score is, I'm not even sure what the game is.
Ashleigh Brilliant

To be sure of hitting the target, shoot first, and call whatever you hit the target.
Ashleigh Brilliant

Chance is always powerful. Let your hook be always cast; in the pool where you least expect it, there will be fish.
Ovid

May the road rise up to greet you, and the wind be always at your back . . . .
Irish Blessing

QUICK QUESTION

Are women's birthday suits double-breasted?

LET'S THINK

Autobiographies should begin with Chapter Two.
after Ellery Sedgwick

While there is a chance of the world getting through its troubles, I hold that a reasonable man has to behave as though he were sure of it. If, at the end, your cheerfulness is not justified, at any rate you will have been cheerful.
H.G. Wells

I'd like to see Paris before I die . . . Philadelphia would do!
W.C. Fields

The more you say, the less people remember. The fewer the words, the greater the profit.
Fenelon

As for me, all I know is that I know nothing.
Socrates

They can conquer who believe they can.
Virgil

INTERESTING FACTOIDS

Walter Cavanaugh, "Mr. Plastic Fantastic," has 1,196 different valid credit cards (but does he owe as much as I do?).

The oldest known goldfish lived until it was 41 years of age. It was called Fred.

A 1,400 year old piece of still-edible cheese was discovered in Ireland, in 1987.

There is a village in Newfoundland, Canada called Dildo.

In Kentucky, 50 percent of those married for the first time are teenagers.

If an orangutan belches at you, beware. He's warning you to stay away from his territory.

Einstein couldn't speak fluently as a child. His parents were afraid he was retarded.

In Los Angeles, there are more automobiles than people.

About one in three Americans flush the toilet while they're still sitting on it.

Cold showers actually increase male sexual arousal.

You're more likely to get stung by a bee when it's windy than in any other type of weather.

You can tell when a gorilla is angry because it will stick its tongue out.

In 1976, a Los Angeles secretary formally married her 50-pound pet rock, probably because it could be relied upon not to wander.

The first sperm banks opened in 1964. One was located in Tokyo and the other in Iowa City.

In 1980, the Yellow Pages accidentally listed a Texas funeral home under frozen foods.

In 1974, 1,200 college students decided to streak at the same time in Boulder, Colorado.

In 1983, a Japanese artist copied the Mona Lisa using only toast.

In 1984, a Canadian farmer began renting ad space on the sides of his cows.

About 96 percent of all American children can now recognize Donald McRonald.

Mosquitoes are attracted to people who have recently eaten bananas. You eat bananas, then they go bananas.

Some penguins can jump 6 feet in the air.

The average human has seven sex fantasies each day. So what are you waiting for?

ON THE ROAD AGAIN: CHICKENS

QUESTION:

Why did the chicken cross the road?

ANSWERS:

Machiavelli

Who cares why? The ends justify whatever motive it had.

Thomas de Torquemada

Give me ten minutes alone with that chicken and I'll make it tell us why.

Timothy Leary

Because that's the only kind of trip this lousy establishment lets it take.

John Locke

It doesn't matter; a chicken's actions have no meaning except to it.

Fox Mulder

It was yet another government conspiracy.

Freud

The fact that you thought that the chicken crossed that road reveals underlying sexual insecurity on your part.

Darwin

Chickens, over geological eras, have been selected naturally so that they are now genetically conditioned to cross any road they see.

Richard M. Nixon

The chicken could not have possibly crossed the road. I repeat, the chicken did not cross that road, or any other road.

Martin Luther King, Jr.

I envision a world where all chickens will be justly free to cross all roads without having their motives called into question.

Immanuel Kant

The chicken, an autonomous being, naturally chose to cross this road of its own free will.

Grandpa

In my day, we didn't ask why the chicken crossed the road. No, when someone told us that the chicken had crossed the road, we believed them. That was good enough for us. There's no respect these days, for chickens or anything else.

Bill Gates

I have just released the new Chicken 4000, which will cross Roads, balance your checkbook, and do your income tax return. Unfortunately, when it divides 3 by 2 it gets 1.499999999999.

M. C. Escher

That depends on which plane of reality the chicken was occupying at the time the road was crossed.

George Orwell

Because the government had brain-washed into thinking that it had its own reason to cross the road, when in fact, it was really only serving their best interests.

Colonel Sanders

I can't believe I missed one.

Plato

Only for the greater good.

Aristotle

To actualize its full potential.

Karl Marx

It was a historical inevitability and it will soon be followed by a mass of chickens.

Albert Einstein

Whether the chicken crossed the road or indeed, whether it was the road that crossed the chicken, depends on your own frame of reference.

The Sphinx

You tell me.

Joseph Stalin

Who cares? Shoot it, I need lunch.

FINANCIAL ADVICE

Two can live as cheaply as one, but only for half as long.

A verbal contract isn't worth the paper it's written on.
Samuel Goldwyn

If you let that sort of thing go on, your bread and butter will be cut right out from under your feet.
Ernest Bevin

Things are more like they are now than they ever were before.
Dwight D. Eisenhower

YET ANOTHER BAD JOKE

A poor man is stranded alone on a desert island. One day, a beautiful blonde, wearing a wet suit and scuba diving equipment walks out of the sea.

She approaches him and asks, "How long has it been since your last cigarette?"

"Ten years!" he answers.

She reaches over, unzips a waterproof pocket on her left sleeve and pulls out a packet of cigarettes and a box of matches. He takes a cigarette, lights it, and after a long drag says, "Man, oh man! Is that good!"

Then she asks him, "How long has it been since your last drink?"

He replies, "Ten years!"

She reaches over, unzips a waterproof pocket on the right sleeve, retrieves a bottle of malt whiskey and gives it to him. He takes a long, hard swallow and says, "Fantastic!"

Then she starts to open a long zipper that runs down the front of her wet suit and as she does, she says to him, "And how long has it been since you've played around?"

At this, he shouts, "Good Lord, don't tell me you've got golf clubs in there too!"

CHANGE IS FOR THOSE WHO CAN'T RESIST IT

The door that encloses a bigoted mind opens outwards so that the only result of the pressure of facts upon it is to close it more snugly.

after Ogden Nash

YOU CAN SAY THAT ONE MORE TIME

No one can make you feel inferior without your consent.

Eleanor Roosevelt

Success seems to be largely a matter of hanging on after others have let go.

William Feather

In the middle of difficulty lies opportunity.

Albert Einstein

It is not the man who has little, but the man who craves more, that is poor.

Seneca

The mode by which the inevitable comes to pass is effort.

Oliver Wendell Holmes

Life affords no higher pleasure than that of surmounting difficulties, passing from one step of success to another, forming new wishes and seeing them gratified.

Samuel Johnson

I feel that the greatest reward for doing is the opportunity to do more.

Jonas Salk

We have always had two classes in this country, the have-nots and the haves. But now, there's a third: the have but haven't paid for yets.

Anon

Infidels in all ages have battled for the rights of man, and have at all times been the fearless advocates of liberty and justice.

Robert Green Ingersoll

All national institutions of churches, whether Jewish, Christian, or Turkish, appear to me no other than human inventions, set up to terrify and enslave mankind, and monopolize power and profit.

Thomas Paine

A RELIGIOUS EXPERIENCE:
UNIQUE DAILY AFFIRMATIONS

As I let go of guilt, I become more in touch with my Inner Sociopath.

I have the power to push my imagination to ever-soaring levels of suspicion and paranoia.

I assume total responsibility for all my actions, with the exception of the ones that are somebody else's fault.

I do not need to punish, deceive or compromise myself. Unless I want to.

In a few cultures, what I do would be considered close to normal.

Having control over myself could be almost as exciting as having control over others.

My intuition clearly makes up for my lack of judgement.

I honor my personality flaws, since they make up the bulk of my personality.

Joan of Arc heard voices too, so why worry?

I am not as judgemental as all those censorious, ignorant self-centered people around me.

Why suffer in silence when you can still moan, shout and complain endlessly?

As I learn the innermost secrets of the people I work with, they reward me in many ways to keep my mouth shut.

When someone injures me, forgiveness is more spiritual than a lawsuit, but it's not nearly as gratifying.

The first step is to say good things about myself. The second, to do good things for myself. The third, is to find someone to buy me good things.

As I learn to trust, I no longer need to carry a gun, but a knife still comes in handy.

All of me is beautiful and valuable, even the fat, ignorant, and disgusting parts.

I am at one or two with my duality.

Blessed are the very flexible, for they can tie themselves into spectacular knots.

I will strive to act each day as if it were my 80th birthday.

Only a lack of imagination prevents me from immobilizing myself with imaginary fears.

I will express every facet of my being, regardless of federal, state, and local laws.

Today I will gladly share my experience and advice with anyone, for there are few sweeter words than "I told you so."

False hope is better than no hope.

A good scapegoat is always as welcome as a solution.

Why should I waste my time reliving the mistakes of the past when I can spend it worrying about those of the future?

The complete lack of evidence is definitely the surest sign that the conspiracy must be working.

I am learning that criticism is not nearly as rewarding as sabotage.

Becoming fully aware of my character defects has lead me to the next step— blaming my parents.

DRINK TO ME ONLY WITH THINE EYES

What contemptible scoundrel has stolen the cork to my lunch?

W.C. Fields

A woman drove me to drink and I didn't even have the decency to thank her.

Anon

Sir, if you were my husband, I would poison your drink.

Lady Astor to Winston Churchill

Madam, if you were my wife, I would drink it.

His reply

Abstainer: a weak person who yields to the temptation of denying himself a pleasure.

Ambrose Bierce

A HEALTHY OLD AGE

My grandmother is well over eighty and still doesn't need glasses. She drinks straight out of the bottle.

after Henny Youngman

IF YOU GET HEADACHES, READ THIS

Albert was a successful university professor, but his research and teaching were hampered increasingly by his terrible headaches. Nothing his doctor prescribed helped and several specialists were baffled. Eventually, after a long series of painful tests, his doctor called him in for a consultation.

"I have good news and bad news," said the doctor.

"The good news is that I can promise you an end to those headaches. The bad news is that it will require castration. You have an extremely rare disorder that presses your testicles against the base of your spine, which in turn causes you terrible headaches. To relieve the pressure, the testicles must go."

Albert was dumbfounded and very depressed. He wanted the headaches to stop, but what a price to pay for relief. Suicide even crossed his mind. After a long internal battle that lasted two weeks, he returned to the doctor and consented to the operation. When it was over he left the hospital in a slightly better frame of mind. What was done was done. Now he would start a new life. As he walked past a men's clothing store, he thought, "A new start really needs a new suit."

So he walked in and said to a salesman, "I'd like a new suit."

The salesman looked him over and replied, "That, sir, will be a size 46 long."

Albert was startled, "How did you know that?" he asked.

"I've seen them all," was the reply.

Albert put on the suit and it was a perfect fit.

As he admired himself in the mirror, the salesman said, "Shirts are on special today. Would you like to see one with a 35 inch sleeve and 15½ inch neck sir?"

"Yes I would," answered Albert, "but how did you know my size?"

"I've seen them all," came back the reply.

Albert put on the shirt. It matched the suit and fitted perfectly. As he was admiring himself, the salesman said, "Would sir like a new pair of shoes?"

Feeling things were going well, Albert agreed.

"Well, sir," said the salesman. "I have a pair of brown, slip-on 8½ Es that would go really well with that suit."

Albert was astonished. "How did you know my shoe size?" he asked.

"I've seen them all," was the reply.

Albert put on the shoes. They were a perfect match for the suit and fitted like a glove. He walked around in them and they were very, very comfortable.

The salesman then enquired, "Can I interest you in a new hat, sir? I've an 8½ inch that will just go perfectly with your new outfit."

"How did . . . .never mind you've seen them all, right?" said Albert.

The salesman nodded.

The hat also was a great success. Just as Albert was about to pay for everything, the salesman said, "Finally, would sir like some new underwear?"

Albert thought for a moment and then decided, why not.

"Let's see," said the salesman, "that'll be size 38."

Albert started to laugh. "No," he replied. "It's size 36. I've been wearing size 36 since I was 21 years old."

"But, sir," said the salesman, "you shouldn't be wearing size 36. It will press your testicles against the base of your spine and give you terrible headaches. Believe me sir, I've seen them all. You must wear size 38."

POINT, COUNTERPOINT

It is said that a long-winded politician cornered the newspaper editor, Horace Greenley, at a convention and confided proudly that he, himself, was a self-made man.

"That, sir," Greenley replied, "relieves the Almighty of a terrible responsibility."

CROSS-EXAMINATIONS

Lawyer: So you admit that, before signing the death certificate, you had not taken the man's pulse?

Doctor: Yes, that is true.

Lawyer: Did you listen for a heartbeat, then?

Doctor: No, I did not.

Lawyer: Did you check to see whether or not, he was breathing?

Doctor: No, I did not.

Lawyer: So even though you signed his death certificate, you hadn't taken any of the necessary steps to ensure he was dead, had you?

Doctor: Well, let me explain it to you this way. The man's brain was sitting in a jar of alcohol on my desk, but I suppose he could still be out there practising law, for all I know.

LIKE THESE?

Silence is the only thing that can't be misquoted.

*Anon (Don't believe it. Exercising your right to
remain silent can be misinterpreted as guilt)*

Pleasant words are as a honeycomb, sweet to the soul, and health to the bones.

Proverbs 16:24

As winter strips the leaves from around us, so that we may see the
distant regions that were formerly concealed, so old age takes away
our enjoyments only to enlarge the prospect of the coming eternity.

Richter

The art of medicine consists of amusing the patient while nature
cures the disease.

Voltaire

Your main obligation is to amuse yourself.

S.J. Perelman

This is a world of action, and not for moping and droning on.

Dickens

You can preach a better sermon with your life than with your lips.

Goldsmith

As scarce as truth is, the supply has always been in excess of the demand.

Josh Billings

Happiness is not a reward—it is the consequence.
Suffering is not a punishment—it is a result.

Robert Ingersoll

Serenity, simplicity, gravity, self control and purity of thought are the austerities
of the mind.

Bhagavad Gita

A great mind becomes a great fortune.

Seneca

REMEMBER

You never get a second chance to make a good first impression.

PUNISHMENTS

A group of chess enthusiasts were staying in a hotel where a tournament was being held. Many of them were standing around in the lobby discussing their recent victories. The manager came out of his office and told them to leave.

"Why?" they asked.

"Because," he said, "I don't like chess nuts boasting in an open foyer."

• • •

A physician regularly visited a pub on his way home and always ordered a hazelnut daiquiri. The bartender was so used to his routine that he prepared the drink and set it up on the bar at 5:25 each evening. One day, as he began to get the drink ready, the bartender found he was out of hazelnut extract. After a moment's thought, he substituted hickory nut extract and set the drink on the bar. The doctor came in, took one sip and exclaimed, "This isn't a hazelnut daiquiri!"

The bartender, a little shaken, replied, "No, I'm sorry, it's a hickory daiquiri, doc."

• • •

A hungry lion came across two men in the jungle. One was reading a book, while the other was typing. The lion pounced on the reader and devoured him. Then he left. Even the king of the jungle knows that readers digest and writers cramp.

• • •

A local newspaper held a pun contest. I sent in ten of them, hoping that one of them would win. Unfortunately, no pun in ten did.

• • •

A woman visits her psychiatrist. "Doctor," she says, "I keep having these alternating dreams. First I'm a wigwam; then I'm a teepee; then a wigwam. Am I going mad? What's the matter with me?"

The doctor thinks a moment and says, "It's nothing serious, you're just two tents."

• • •

A patient complained to his dentist that his new upper plate was hurting. The dentist examined it and found it badly eroded.

"What have you been eating?" he asked the patient.

"Well," came the reply, "my wife makes wonderful Hollandaise sauce and I've been putting it on fish, meat, vegetables, virtually everything. Could it be that?"

The dentist nodded his head. "It's eaten right through the upper plate. I'll have to have another made, but this time we'll use chrome."

"Why chrome?" asked the patient.

"It's obvious," said the dentist, "there's no plate like chrome for the Hollandaise!"

IN MY OPINION

I want nothing to do with any religion concerned with keeping the masses satisfied to live in hunger, filth, and ignorance. I want nothing to do with any order, religious or otherwise, which does not teach people that they are capable of becoming happier and more civilized, on this earth, capable of becoming true man, master of his fate and captain of his soul.

William Ernest Henley

POSSESSED

Too many of us define who we are by our possessions, what we have, what we wear, the kind of house we live in and the automobile we drive. If you think of yourself as the one with the gold watch with the flashy sportscar, a house fire will destroy, not only your possessions, but yourself.

after Linda Henley

SPEAK UP

On their first date, Bill took Mary to the carnival. When they arrived, Bill asked her if there was anything she really wanted to do.

"Get weighed," she replied.

So Bill took her to a man with a scale who tried to guess her weight. He missed it by 4 pounds and so gave her a gift.

Bill and Mary then went for a ride on the roller coaster. When it was over, he asked her what she wanted to do next and was surprised when she answered, "Get weighed."

This time, there was no prize, since the owner of the scale recognized her. They then went for a ride on the bumper cars. After they got off, Bill asked Mary what she wanted to do next.

"Get weighed," she answered.

At this, Bill decided there was something very odd about her and decided to quickly end the evening, leaving her outside her front door, with only a quick handshake.

Mary's roommate was awaiting her return and asked her how the evening had gone.

"Wousy!" she replied.

I HAVE BEEN TOLD THE IMPORTANCE OF PUNCTUATION

Woman without her man is savage.
Woman: without her, man is savage.

Thanx John!

TO THE POINT

Great art appeals to the soul.

Anon

You grow up the day you have your first real laugh at yourself.

Ethel Barrymore

If you want a rainbow, you gotta put up with the rain.

Anon

He don't know and he don't know that he don't know!

Anon (Comment on an old examination paper of mine)

BY WHOSE STANDARDS?

Most Intelligent Animals

1. Man (women included).
2. Chimpanzee (so my parents meant it lovingly when they called me a little chimp??).
3. Gorilla.
4. Orangutan.
5. Gibbon.
6. Baboon.
7. Monkey.
8. Smaller-toothed Whale.
9. Dolphin.
10. Elephant

Interestingly enough, Cat is 2042 on the list, right after Common Dung Beetle, but before Tax Collector. Only joking; no audit, please.

SANTA CLAUS: TELLING THE BRUTAL TRUTH

(IT'S IMPORTANT FOR YOUR CHILDREN TO UNDERSTAND THIS JOKE)

Given the fact that millions of Americans believe a Canadian is smuggling toys into the United States from the North Pole on an annual basis, U.S. Customs and Excise has decided to examine the Santa Claus phenomenon in detail.
Our findings are presented below:

1. We have been unable to identify any species of flying reindeer. However, there are hundreds of thousands of species yet to be identified, not to mention aliens, bigfoot, etc. For this reason, we cannot completely rule out reindeer that may be able to fly, but we are certainly skeptical.

2. There are 2 billion people on earth under the age of 18. Since, however, Santa Claus does not usually provide Christmas gifts to Jewish, Hindu, Buddhist or Muslim children, that leaves 378 million to receive toys on Christmas Eve. At an average of 3.5 children per household, that's 91.8 million chimneys to descend.

3. Given the different time zones and the earth's rotation, assuming he travels from east to west, Santa will have 31 hours of Christmas. This indicates he must make 822.6 housecalls per second. Assuming at least one good child per household, Santa has approximately 1/1000th of a second to park his sleigh, hop out, climb down the chimney, fill the stockings, put presents under the tree, eat the snacks left for him, get back up the chimney to his sleigh and drive it to the next house. If we make the admittedly false assumption that these houses are evenly distributed around the earth, we're talking about 0.78 miles between chimney descents, a total distance of 75.5 million miles. This doesn't give Santa any time for pit stops. He'll probably need plenty because of all the snacks, drinks and other goodies he's forced to eat to avoid hurting children's feelings. This means Santa's sleigh will have to move at speeds of some 650 miles per second, or 3000 times the speed of sound. This must be tiring for the reindeer, which normally can run at a top speed of 15 miles per hour.

4. Assuming that each child gets toys weighing no more than a doll or a train set (about two pounds), the sleigh must carry 321,300 tons, not counting Santa's weight. He is known to be a little on the heavy side (who wouldn't be after all those snacks?). A normal reindeer can pull about 300 pounds over the snow. Even if we assume that, in the air, a flying reindeer can pull ten times that load, Santa will need about 214,200 reindeer to move his sleigh. This increases the weight of the sleigh to approximately 353,430 tons, or four times that of the Queen Elizabeth! (The ship, not the monarch).

5. A payload of 353,000 tons, travelling at 650 miles per second, will meet with enormous air resistance, causing great heat. In fact, the leading pair of reindeer will have to absorb 14.3 quintillion joules of energy per second. Unfortunately, given the composition of reindeer, they will inevitably catch fire, exposing those behind them. This process of spontaneous combustion, caused by excessive friction, will create an enormous sonic boom. Not only will the entire reindeer team be vaporized, but poor old Santa will be subjected to centrifugal effects 17,500.06 times higher than that caused by gravity, pinning him to the back of his sleigh with a 4,315,015 pound force. Given his overweight and his excess sugar and fat consumption, this would not be good for his health.

We have decided, therefore, that, since these toys are gifts, they should not be subjected to duties and Santa should be allowed to continue his good work without being subjected to further stress by the U.S. Customs and Excise.

NOT TOO SMART

Brian Johnson, 28, who had been charged with a string of vending machine robberies, tried to post his $500 bail in dimes.

• • •

Alan Tostman, 39, was arrested in Miami Beach, Florida after allegedly knocking out an armored car driver and stealing four bags of money.
These turned out to contain $800 in PENNIES and weighed 30 pounds each.
He was arrested easily by police officers, who found him staggering down the street.

• • •

English was good enough for Jesus Christ and it's good enough for the children of Texas.

Miriam "Ma" Ferguson, Governor of Texas, 1924

• • •

I stopped believing in Santa Claus when my mother took me to see him in a department store, and he asked for my autograph.

Shirley Temple

• • •

Drug-possession defendant Albert Hannes, on trial in June in Portland, Oregon, said he had been searched without a warrant. The prosecutor replied the officer didn't need a warrant because a "bulge" in Albert's jacket could have been a gun.

"Nonsense," said Albert, who happened to be wearing the same jacket to court.

He handed it over, so the judge could examine it more closely. The judge discovered a packet of cocaine in the pocket and laughed so much he needed a five-minute recess to compose himself.

LAUGHTER: SAD BUT TRUE

Millionaires seldom laugh.

Andrew Carnegie
(unless, of course, they are reading this book)

THINK ABOUT THIS

To die for an idea is to place a pretty high price upon conjecture.

Anatole France

TRANSLATE THIS

Quidquid latine dictum sit, altum viditur.
(*Clue: Anything in Latin sounds profound.*)

GOOD NIGHT

Finish every day and be done with it. You have done
what you could; some blunders and absurdities have
crept in—forget them as soon as you can. Tomorrow
is a new day. You shall begin it well and serenely,
and with too high a spirit to be encumbered with
your old nonsense.

Ralph Waldo Emerson

PRETTY BAD JOKE

A young man applied for a job in a huge department
store and was given a one day sales trial. The day was long and arduous, but
finally 6 o'clock came around.

"How many people did you sell to today?"

"One," said the young salesman.

"Only one," blurted out the boss, "Most of my staff here make 20 or 30 sales a
day. How much was that sale worth?"

"Four hundred thousand dollars," replied the young man.

"How did you manage that?" asked his flabbergasted boss.

"Well," said the salesman, "this man came in and I sold him a small packet of
fishing hooks, then a packet of medium hooks and finally a packet of really large
hooks. Then I sold him a 10 pound fishing line, a 25 pound one and a 150 pound
one. I asked him where he was going fishing and he said about 100 miles down
the coast. I suggested he'd probably need a boat, so I took him down to the boat
department and sold him that 20 foot schooner with the twin engines. Then he
said his automobile probably wouldn't be able to tow it, so I took him to the car
department and sold him a new four-wheel drive truck."

His boss took three steps backwards and asked in amazement, "You sold all that
to a guy who came in here for a packet of small fish hooks?"

"No," answered the potential salesman. "He came in to buy a box of aspirins for
his wife and I said to him, 'Your weekend's shot, you may as well go fishing.'"

A FEW MORE INSIGHTS

One good turn gets most of the blankets.

It is not what a teenager knows that bothers his parents, it's how he found out.

There are two kinds of pedestrians—the quick and the dead.

Everybody wants to go to Heaven, but nobody wants to die.

After eating, do amphibians have to wait an hour before getting out of the water?

If white wine goes with fish, do white grapes go with sushi?

When sign makers go on strike, what do they write on their picket signs?

Why isn't there mouse-flavored cat food?

Why is it that when you transport something by car, it's called a shipment, but when you transport something by ship, it's called cargo?

When your pet bird sees you reading the newspaper, does he wonder why you're just sitting there, staring at carpeting?

THINGS TO LEARN FROM MY DOG "CHAMP"

When someone you love comes home, run happily to greet them.

Make sure anyone who invades your territory knows about it.

Play with your friends.

Loyalty is essential.

Don't pretend to be what you're not.

Thrive on attention and enjoy being petted.

Try to growl first; bite only if that doesn't work.

When the weather's hot, drink plenty and lie in the shade.

Delight in the joy of walking.

When a friend is having a bad day, keep quiet, sit close by and gently nuzzle her.

Eat your meals and show appreciation for them.

Take naps when you get the chance.

NEWS RELEASE

NEW ELEMENT DISCOVERED!

The heaviest known element was discovered recently by material researchers at the Institute for Material Insight, University of Berkeley. Tentatively named Administratium, this element has no protons or electrons and, therefore, has an atomic weight of 0. Despite this, one neutron, 135 assistant neutrons, 82 vice-neutrons, and 123 assistant vice-neutrons have been identified. These 341 particles are held together in a nucleus by a force that involves the endless interchange of particles called memoranda. Since it lacks electrons, Administratium is inert. It's major property is its ability to impede any activity it comes into contact with. To illustrate, Administratium added to most reactions can slow their completion time by a factor of 100.

Administratium has a half-life of approximately three years. Throughout this time, although it has the smell and appearance of decay, this does not actually occur. At approximately three year intervals, a structural reorganization takes place, however, during which the neutron, vice neutrons, and assistant neutrons exchange places. After each such reorganization, despite continuing inertia, the atomic mass increases.

Administratium tends to concentrate and proliferate in large corporations, government agencies and universities, in new luxurious and well-maintained buildings, even if all the surrounding infrastructure is run down and dilapidated.

There is no doubt that this element is highly toxic and is capable of destroying all productive reactions. It is especially dangerous if combined with Lawyeridium and/or Accountantium. Attempts to identify methods of controlling the negative effects of Administratium so far have been largely unsuccessful.

HOCKEY(E)

Al Josephson played in the American Hockey League. Unfortunately, during one violent match, he was hit in the left eye with a high stick and lost all sight in that eye. A couple of weeks later, it had been replaced with a glass one and he returned to his team. About a month after that, he was taken hard into the boards and, during the collision, his glass eye popped out. The game was stopped, the ice searched and the eye returned to Josephson by the referee.

"It takes guts to play with only one good eye," said the official. "What would happen if you got hit in it with a stick or a puck?"

Without missing a beat, Josephson responded, "I love this game. If I become completely blind, I'd just have to become a referee."

AN INTIMATE RELATIONSHIP

John is attracted to a woman called Anne. He asks her out to a movie; she accepts; they have a very good time. A few nights later, he invites her to dinner, and again they have a pleasant evening. They continue to see each other quite regularly, and soon neither is seeing anyone else.

And then, as they are driving home from the theatre, a thought occurs to Anne and she says aloud, "Do you know that, as of tonight, we've been going out together for exactly six months?" And then there is silence in the car, a very loud silence.

Anne asks herself: I wonder if that bothers him? Maybe he's feeling constrained by our relationship; maybe he thinks I'm pushing him into an obligation he doesn't want, or isn't sure about. And John is thinking: Is it really 6 months?

And Anne is thinking: I'm not sure I really need this type of relationship, either. Sometimes, I wish I had a little more space. I mean, where are we going? Will we just keep seeing each other, or are we heading towards marriage? Children? A lifetime together? Am I ready for that degree of commitment? Do I really know what this person is really like?

And John is thinking: . . . so that means it was . . . let's see . . . April when we started going together, right after I had the car serviced, which means, . . . Let me see the odometer . . . whoa! It's way overdue for its oil change.

And Anne is thinking: He's distraught. I can see pain on his face. Maybe I'm reading this all wrong. Maybe he wants more commitment, greater intimacy; maybe he sensed—even before I did—that I had reservations. I bet that's the problem. That's why he's so reluctant to express his feelings. He's afraid of rejection.

And John is thinking: They're going to have to look at that transmission again. I don't care what those half-wits say, it's still not shifting the way it should. And they better not try to blame it on the cold weather again. What cold weather? It's 85 degrees out, and this thing is still shifting like an old school bus, and I paid those incompetent thieves $950.

And Anne is thinking: He's so angry. And I can't really blame him. I'd be angry too. I feel very guilty putting him through this, but it's not my fault, I can't help the way I feel. I'm just not sure yet, that's all.

And John is thinking: They'll probably claim there was only a 90-day warranty. That's exactly what will happen, the rip-off artists.

And Anne is thinking: Maybe I'm just too idealistic, always waiting for that knight to come riding up on his white horse. Here I am, sitting next to a perfectly decent person, one I enjoy being with, one who I care for, and one who truly cares for me. A man who is in pain just because of my self-centered, immature romantic fantasy.

And John is thinking: Warranty? They'll demand a warranty? I'll give them a warranty. They can take their warranty and stick it right up their . . .

"John," Anne finally says aloud.

"What?" says John, startled by the sudden interruption to his train of thought.

"Don't torture yourself like this," she says, her eyes filling with tears. "I should never . . . oh God, I feel so . . . ." (she breaks down, weeping)

"What?" says John.

"I'm a fool," Anne sobs. "I know there's no knight. Believe me, I really know that. There's no knight, and there's no white horse."

"There's no white horse?" asks John, completely taken aback.

"You think I'm foolish, don't you?" Anne says.

"No!" says John, delighted to finally know one correct answer.

"It's just . . . it's that I . . . I need more time," Anne replies.

There is a 20 second pause while John tries desperately to come up with a safe response, any safe response that might work.

"Yes," he says.

"Oh John, do you really, truly feel that way?" she asks.

"What way?" replies John.

"That way about time," says Anne.

"Oh," says John. "Yes, yes I do."

Anne turns to face him, gazing deeply into his eyes. He starts to become very nervous about what she might say next, especially if it involves a white horse. Eventually, she speaks.

"Thank you, John," she says.

"Thank you," says John, even more confused than ever.

He then takes her home, and she lies on her bed, a conflicted, tortured soul, where she weeps for hours. When John gets back to his apartment, he opens a bag of chips, turns on the TV, and becomes deeply engrossed in a darts match between two Scots he has never even heard of. A tiny voice deep in the recesses of his mind tells him something major occurred during the drive from the theatre, but he is sure he would never understand what and he decides it's better not to think about it.

The next day, Anne will call one, or perhaps two of her closest friends, and they will discuss the situation for weeks. For hours, in painstaking detail, they will analyze everything she said and his responses, going over it time and time again, exploring every word, facial expression, and gesture for significance, searching for each and every ramification. They will continue to discuss this subject, off and on, for weeks, maybe months, never reaching any definite conclusions.

Meanwhile, John, while working on his automobile with a mutual friend of both he and Anne, will pause, frown, and say, "When did Anne own a white horse?"

DIG THIS: ONE UP

I am told that there really is an eccentric who digs things out of his backyard and sends them to the Smithsonian Institute, labeled with scientific names, insisting that they are actual archeological or paleontological finds. The weird thing about the letter that follows is that this guy probably exists and does this in his spare time! True or not, this letter is very funny.

Paleoanthropology Division
Smithsonian Institute
207 Pennsylvania Avenue
Washington, DC 20078

Dear Sir:

Thank you for your latest submission to our Division, labeled "318-C, layer three, next to dog kennel—Hominid skull." We have examined this interesting specimen in some detail and regret to inform you that we are forced to disagree with your hypothesis that it provides "conclusive proof of the presence of an early ancestor of Man in Orange County, over 3 million years ago." Rather, it appears to be the head of a doll. One of our staff, who has several small children, has identified it as from a "Malibu Darby." We are sorry to contradict your findings, since we are aware you have put considerable effort into your research. However, in support of our position, we would like to point out a series of physical attributes of the specimen which might have tipped you off about its relatively modern origin.

1. Ancient hominid remains are typically fossilized bone. Your specimen is made of molded plastic.

2. The specimen has a cranial capacity of only 3.5 cubic centimeters, well below the minimum found in even the earliest proto-hominids.

3. The dentition pattern evident on the skull which you attribute to "wild, man-eating Pliocene clams" appears to us to be more consistent with the teeth of the common domesticated canine.

Without going into any greater detail, let me summarize by pointing out that the specimen seems to be the head of a Darby doll, bitten off by the household dog. Clams don't have teeth.

It is with feelings of regret that we must also deny your request to radio-carbon date the specimen. There are two fundamental reasons for this. Firstly, our laboratory is loaded very heavily with other pressing research needs which, unfortunately, must be given priority. Secondly, since the first Darby dolls were manufactured in 1956 AD, any date resulting from radio-carbon dating would have confidence limits that would be wildly inaccurate. Sadly, your request that we approach the National Science Foundation's Phylogeny

Department to assign the specific name "Californicus riperhead-off" to your specimen has been voted down. I, for one, fought strongly in support of this idea, but ultimately this taxonomy was rejected because of the hyphen in the species name and the fact that the Latin was rather irregular.

Nevertheless, amid all this negative news, I am happy to report that the Institute accepts your kind donation of the specimen. While it may not be the hominid fossil you had hoped for, it is still an excellent example of the great body of work of a similar nature that you are achieving. You should be aware that the Director is so impressed with your efforts that he has a special shelf, in his own office, that is now used to display this and other specimens you have so kindly presented to the Institute. We are all awaiting with keen interest the additional finds that are likely to appear from the ongoing excavations in your backyard. We eagerly await your planned visit to Washington and several of our staff are pressing the Director to pay for it out of the Institute's travel budget. In particular, we should like to hear, in more detail, your theory on the "transmutating of scintillating ferrous ions in a structural intermatrix" that you used to explain why the possible juvenile Tyrannosaurus Rex femur you recently sent us looks so much like a very rusty 10mm automotive crescent wrench.

Yours in Science,
Arnold Bennett, Curator, Antiquities

LAST SEEN WEARING....

Date when species was last seen alive:

1. Aurochs (Wild Great Ox)	1627
2. Aepyornis (Giant Elephant Bird from Madagascar)	1649
3. Dodo (Need I say more)	1681
4. Sterller's sea cow (Big Freakin' Cow that swims)	1768
5. Great Auk (Big Sea Bird)	1844
6. Tarpan (Big Ol' Dead Horse)	1851
7. Quagga (A strange Zebra-like creature)	1883
8. Guadalupe Island Caracara (Large brown hawk)	1900
9. Passenger Pigeon (Pigeon)	1914
10. Carolina Parakeet (Bird)	1918

BUSINESS NEWS FROM THE NORTH POLE

Home shopping channels, mail-order catalogues, and toy superstores have cut
deeply into the dominance of Happy Christmas Inc.'s gift distribution business.
Restructuring has become inevitable and Donner and Blitzen unfortunately have
been let go. This reindeer downsizing has been made feasible through the short
term leasing of a late model sled from Mitsutashi Inc., a leading Japanese
transportation company. Available for only 48 hours each year, this sled is
for the exclusive use of the CEO, doing his annual delivery run. Improved
productivity is anticipated from Dasher and Dancer, both of whom took a
refresher course at the Harvest Business School during the summer.
Rudolph will not be let go, although he has been undergoing treatment for
substance abuse. Calling Rudolph "a lush who was always into the sauce and
couldn't pull his own weight," however, was an unfortunate, disruptive comment
and the elf making it now is looking elsewhere for employment.

Other changes also can be expected in our subsidiary, Twelve Days of Christmas
Inc. Although the partridge is being retained, the pear tree has never produced
the anticipated cash crop and is being replaced by a synthetic tree. The gardener
is being let go. The two turtle doves represented an unnecessary redundancy
and their office romance was the cause of several complaints by co-workers.
We are sorry to report their services no longer are required. Under pressure
from Quebec, we have decided to retain the services of the three French hens.
The four calling birds have been replaced by an automated voice mail system,
with call waiting and call forwarding options. Since company telephone bills
have been excessive, an investigation is ongoing into who and how often, these
birds have been calling.

The five gold rings clearly are an error, which became especially obvious after
the Indonesian mine fiasco. Maintaining a portfolio based on one commodity is
not resilient and greater diversification is required. It seems likely that T-Bills,
other precious metals and high technology stocks will be acquired. Perhaps one
gold ring would not be excessive.

Six geese-a-laying is a luxury that the company can ill-afford, especially since
the market for goose eggs has been stagnant for years. These geese will be let go
and cloning will be examined as an option to laying.

The seven swans-a-swimming is a PR gimmick that clearly has lost most of its
appeal. This number was chosen in better times and food bills are now
excessive. Robotic swans are being tested, although eventually computer-
generated alternatives may prove more cost effective. The current swans are
being retrained to learn new strokes before being outplaced.

The eight maids-a-milking concept is seen by many as a deliberate attempt to
unbalance the workforce and is under scrutiny by the EEOC. The militant milk

maids consider this a dead end job and are demanding more upward mobility. The purchase of a milking machine may free them for a-mulching and a-baking. If these tasks do not prove economic, they will be let go.

Nine ladies dancing is an unusual activity and an odd number. The financial return is low. As these individuals age, they are becoming more unwilling to learn new, more popular dance routines. While still on staff, their positions are far from guaranteed. A similar observation can be made of the ten Lords-a-leaping. This clearly is overkill. Lords are expensive, especially since they insist on travelling everywhere first class. There is some talk of replacing them with out-of-work congressmen but these too are known to be very expensive to keep in the style to which they have become accustomed.

Eleven pipers playing and twelve drummers drumming is an obvious case of the band growing too large for its bookings. They are being replaced by a one person band with a synthesizer. New music will be cut back. Obviously, personnel changes should all improve the bottom line. Although incomplete,

studies also indicate that, if instead of spreading shipments over twelve days, all deliveries took place simultaneously, major savings could be made in shipping costs. To this end we are considering changing this subsidiary's name to Christmas Day Inc.

In conclusion, although the Snowe Wright Division in unaffected by this round of reorganization, unless profits improve, the Board may be forced to examine whether seven dwarfs are really required, or whether the number is excessive.

DID YOU NOTICE THIS?

A conclusion occurs at the point at which you run out of new ideas.

For each and every action, there is an equal and opposite criticism.

Until you make a mistake, nobody is listening.

The shorter your arm, the more severe the itch.

She who hesitates is almost certainly right.

DID YOU KNOW?

The average person is about a quarter of an inch taller at night than during the day.

A sneeze zooms out of your mouth at over 600 mph.

The condom, made originally of linen, was invented in the early 1500's.

The first known contraceptive was crocodile dung, used by Egyptians in 2000 B.C. Probably removed a little something from the experience!

Watch out for flying hockey pucks, they can travel at speeds up to 100 mph.

America's first nudist organization was founded in 1929, by 3 men. I suppose they decided to let it all hang out.

Ninety-eight percent of American drivers think they drive better than anyone else. The other 2% are probably in the hospital.

The Neanderthal's brain was bigger than yours is. Yours, not mine.

An Indian woman can legally wed a goat. This is true in North America but usually the goats are old there.

The average bank teller loses $250 every year. Why can't it go into my account?

Howdy Doody had 48 freckles.

What color was Christopher Columbus' hair? Blonde. I expected white, by the time he reached North America.

In 1980, there was only one country in the world with no telephones—Bhutan. The sales of beepers were slow, too.

The largest number of extras ever used in a movie was 300,000, in the film Gandhi.

Every person has a unique tongue print. Don't lick the stamps on your poisoned-pen letters.

Your right lung takes in more air than your left one does. Is this good, or bad? It depends on whether or not you live in Los Angeles.

Women's hearts beat faster than men's (especially when they are in close proximity to me).

Pollsters claim that 40% of dog and cat owners carry pictures of their pets in their wallets. The rest, probably carry pictures of their spouses or grandchildren. What a drag!

Bubble gum contains rubber. Looking at my tires, the reverse is probably true.

You can only smell 1/20th as well as a dog. Sometimes, this is a blessing.

In high school, Robin Williams was voted "Least Likely to Succeed." And look what happened to him. How right they were! Sorry Robin, just joking; don't sue.

Only 55% of all Americans know that the sun is a star.

An estimated 6,000 American teenagers lose their virginity every day. It's not the same 6,000.

Someone paid $14,000 for the bra Marilyn Monroe wore in "Some Like It Hot." Thanks for the mammaries.

ADVICE FROM THE WISE

Never knock on Death's door. Just ring the bell and run. Death really hates that.

Anon

The mind is not a vessel to be filled but a fire to be kindled.

Plutarch

They are able because they think they are able.

Virgil

OUT OF THE MOUTHS OF BABES . . .

It was dry, so very dry. The Mid-west farming community was experiencing the worst drought in its history. A meeting was called at the church to pray for rain. One man brought his small son, who was puzzled by the whole exercise.

"Daddy, daddy," he asked, "why are we in church on a Wednesday? What is everybody doing?"

His father explained about the drought and the need for rain. The little boy looked around again and said, "Daddy, why doesn't anybody have an umbrella?"

STRANGE, BUT TRUE

A horse and a chicken are playing in a field. Unfortunately, the horse becomes careless and falls into a mud hole. As he begins to sink, he begs the chicken to fetch the farmer. The chicken runs to the farmhouse, but can't find him, so she drives the farmer's luxury sportscar to the mud hole. There she ties a rope around its bumper, throws the other end to the sinking horse and by driving the car forward, saves her friend.

A week later, the chicken gets careless and falls into the same mud hole. She yells to the horse to go for the farmer. The horse replies, "Don't worry. I can straddle that mudhole."

So he stretches across the hole and says, "Okay, grab my 'thingy' and pull yourself out of the mud."

This the chicken does and quickly reaches safety.

The moral of this story is simply this; if you're hung like a stallion, you don't need a fancy sportscar to pick up chicks.

BUT DOES IT RHYME?

It was the final day of the International Poetry Contest. The last two remaining contestants squared off. One was a Harvard law graduate from an uppercrust family. The other finalist was from the Northwest Bronx's College of Technology.

The contest had few rules. Each competitor was given two minutes to compose a four-line poem that had to contain Timbuktu. The Harvard graduate went first. Less than sixty seconds after the clock was started he leapt up and recited the poem which follows:

> *Slowly across the endless sand,*
> *Trekked the dusty caravan.*
> *Loaded camels, two by two*
> *Destination—Timbuktu.*

There was pandemonium. The crowd was on its feet, calling for more. How could the redneck from the Bronx improve on that? Again the clock started, and, with a second or two left, the New Yorker jumped up and recited the following:

> *Tim and I, a-hiking went.*
> *Met three whores in a nylon tent.*
> *They were three, and we were two,*
> *So I bucked one and Timbuktu.*

DOES THIS SMART?

Once in a century a man may be ruined or made insufferable by praise. But surely once in a minute something generous dies for want of it.

John Masefield

Any coward can fight if he's sure of winning, but give me the man with the courage to fight, when loss is inevitable. That's my way, sir; and there are many victories worse than a defeat.

after George Eliot

There can be no reconciliation without open warfare. There must first be a brave boisterous battle, with pennants blowing in the wind and cannons roaring, before there can be peace treaties and an enthusiastic shaking of hands.

after Mary Elizabeth Braddon

I have never found in a long experience of politics that criticism is ever inhibited by ignorance.

Harold Macmillan

Not everything that counts can be counted, and not everything that can be counted, counts.

Oscar Wilde

It is not because things are difficult that we do not dare; it is because we do not dare that they are difficult.

Seneca

The world has achieved brilliance without conscience. Ours is a world of nuclear giants and ethical infants.

General Omar Bradley

Always remember that one cloud cannot block out the sun for long.

Anon

Nobody ever means to fall in love. But it happens when love brands itself onto your brain. It's like a new street appearing overnight in the city you've lived in for your whole life. This street is one way and you can't turn around and get off it. It curves up ahead so that you can only see far enough to know that you're heading into the unknown.

Anon

HOW DOES YOUR TEACHING STACK UP?

This class was a religious experience. I had to take everything on faith.

Somebody with a knowledge of English should proofread the textbook.

Despite some students' claims that the textbook was useless, I found it excellent for killing cockroaches.

Help! I'm asleep and I can't wake up.

He's a brilliant lecturer; well organized, lucid and entertaining. He creates great interest in the subject matter. I hope that this positive evaluation doesn't damage his chances of getting tenure.

The lecturer improved as the class wore on. I think this is because he drank more heavily and started to loosen up.

Information was presented like water from a punctured fire hose—spraying in every direction, with no way to stop it.

She teaches like Speedy Gonzalez on a caffeine overdose.

THINK AGAIN

It is never possible to gain from another's loss, or to lose from another's gain.
> *after Martin Bell (Didn't this guy ever play poker?)*

Unless the reformer can invent something which substitutes attractive virtues for attractive vices, he will fail.
> *Walter Lippmann*

He who ignores discipline despises himself, but whoever heeds correction gains understanding.
> *Proverbs 15:32*

That essence of class, subtlety.
> *after Aaron Bowden*

Of all treasons against humanity, there is no one worse than he who employs great intellectual force to keep down the intellect of his less favored brothers.
> *William Ellery Channing*

BAD NEWS

THE WORLD'S MOST ENDANGERED MAMMALS

Species	Number Left
1. Tasmanian Devil	?
2. Halcom Fruit Bat	?
3. Ghana fat mouse	?
4. Kouprey	10
5. Javan Rhinoceros	50
6. Iriomate cat	60
7. Black Lion Tamarin	130
8. Pygmy Hog	150
9. Tamaraw	200
10. Indus Dolphin	400

GOOD NEWS

LONGEST LIVED SPECIES (EXCLUDING HUMANS)

Species	Max. Age in Years
1. Quahog (marine clam)	up to 200
2. Giant Tortoise	150
3. Greek Tortoise	110
4. Killer Whale	90
5. European Eel	88
6. Lake sturgeon	82
7. Sea Anemone	80
8. Elephant	78
9. Freshwater mussel	75
10. Andean Condor	70

DIETARY PROBLEMS

If you're having trouble losing weight, then try
the seafood diet. See food, eat it.

WEDDED BLISS

As she listens to the Wedding March, three things are
always foremost in the mind of any bride:
aisle, altar, hymn.

Love is an ideal thing, marriage a real thing; a
confusion of the real with the ideal never goes
unpunished.

Goethe

Marriage is like a cage; one sees the birds
outside desperate to get in, and those inside
to get out.

Montaigne

A honeymoon ought to be like a dining
room table: four bare legs and no drawers.

A LIFE OF SLICE

An avid golfer can't help slicing his ball to the left. Naturally, this has a very
negative effect on his handicap. One day, at the eleventh hole, the situation
comes to a head. While trying to drive the ball down the fairway, he slices it
over the hedge and onto a busy street. It bounces once and then goes through
the window of a bus, hitting its driver on the head, causing him to black out.
The bus swerves across the road and crashes into a mini-van full of school
children. This catches fire. Six children are badly hurt. The police investigate,
but decline to lay charges against the golfer, classifying the episode as an
unfortunate accident. Night after night, however, the golfer is haunted by a
nightmare that replays the awful event in vivid detail.

About a month later, unable to stand these bad dreams any longer, he visits a
psychiatrist.

"Doctor," he says, "I have this terrible problem. Not long ago, at the eleventh
hole, I sliced my ball onto the street, hitting a bus driver, seriously injuring six
children."

The physician replies, "I play a little golf myself. You must be slicing to the left.
That's not such a problem. I noticed when you came in, you have a slight limp.
Your right leg must be about an inch longer than your left. When you use your
driver, just bend your right leg slightly."

CAN YOU ACCOUNT FOR THIS?

Three engineers and three accountants happen to be on the same train, travelling to different conferences in the same city. At the station, all three accountants buy tickets, but the engineers only get one among them.

"How do you think the three of you are going to travel all that way on one ticket?" asks an accountant.

"Keep your eyes open and you'll learn," answers one of the engineers.

They all board the train. While the accountants each take a seat, the three engineers crowd into a restroom. Shortly after the train leaves the station, a conductor comes around to punch tickets. He knocks on the restroom door and calls, "Your ticket, please! It's the conductor."

The door opens a crack and an arm emerges holding a ticket. The conductor punches it, hands it back and moves on.

The accountants watch this performance and agree it's a great way to save money. So when they are ready to return, after their conference is over, they decide to buy only one ticket themselves. To their astonishment, the engineers, who also are returning home, don't buy any tickets.

"How do you think the three of you are going to travel all that way without a ticket?" asks one of the accountants.

"Keep your eyes open and you'll learn," answers one of the engineers.

When the train arrives, the three accountants pile into one restroom and the three engineers into another nearby. Shortly afterwards, an engineer creeps out of his restroom and knocks on the door of the other one, shouting "Your ticket, please! It's the conductor."

The door opens a crack and an accountant gives him their ticket.

REDUCING YOUR RISKS

If 75% of all accidents happen within 5 miles of home, why not move 10 miles away? Be on the safe side and move 20!

I CLAIM THIS ONE

Half of most people's problems are due to their lack of business knowledge— knowledge of what is their business and what is none of their business.

Gary Tooze

FAIR ENOUGH

Man is born to live and not to prepare to live.

Boris Pasternak

The important thing is never to stop questioning.

Albert Einstein (What was that again?)

REMEMBER THIS

Any new idea is delicate and can be killed by a yawn or a sneer; it can be assassinated by a joke or worried to death by a frown on the right person's brow.

after Charles Brower

Happiness lies, first of all, in health.

George William Curtis

IN REMEMBRANCE

If you would not be forgotten, as soon as you are dead and rotten, either write things worth reading, or do things worth writing.

Ben Franklin

Genealogy is based on the clearly absurd belief that there is no such bird as a cuckold.

Harold D. Foster

PROFOUND QUESTION

Do you agree that New Jersey is the funniest state in the union?

Compare:

He had a wart the size of Kansas.

He had a wart the size of South Dakota.

He had a wart the size of Hawaii.

He had a wart the size of New Jersey.

It may be a three-syllable thing . . . but Florida isn't very funny, it's something about New Jersey . . . .

POLITICAL INSIGHTS

It's dangerous for a national candidate to say things that
people might remember.

Eugene McCarthy

Get all the fools on your side and you can be elected to anything.

Frank Dane

In politics if you want anything said, ask a man; if you
want anything done, ask a woman.

Margaret Thatcher

This is a great day for France!

*Richard Nixon, while attending
Charles De Gaulle's funeral*

Life is one long process of getting tired!

Samuel Butler

Half of our mistakes in life arise from thinking when we
ought to feel and feeling when we ought to think.

Anon

Life can only be understood backwards, but it must be lived forwards.

Soren Kierkegaard

Experience is such a marvellous thing, it enables you to recognize a mistake . . .
when you make it again.

after F. P. Jones

SMART

Every man has his secret sorrows which the world knows not; and often times we
call a man cold when he is only sad.

Henry Wadsworth Longfellow

COMPASSION

If we could read the secret history of our enemies, we should find in each man's
life sorrow and suffering enough to disarm all hostility.

Longfellow

SHAPE UP, OR SHIP OUT

George was a bright youngster, but he had no intention of wasting his time studying. No matter what books, CD-ROMS, or private tutors George was provided with, his grades remained way below average. Finally, after all else had failed, his parents decided to enrol him in a private Catholic school: nuns, weekly mass, the whole religious experience.

When George returned home after the first day, he went straight to his room and, without any prompting, began his homework. He toiled away for three hours, his text books strewn around. Then he emerged for a few minutes for dinner, cleaning his plate rapidly before returning to his room for further study.

This pattern continued, day in day out, until the end of semester. On the last afternoon, George brought home an envelope, which he dropped on the dining room table. His parents opened it and were delighted to see bright red A's under every subject and an A+ in Arithmetic.

Thrilled at this remarkable progress they rushed up to their boy's room.

"George," said his mother. "Why the wonderful academic improvement? Was it the textbooks? The teacher? The new curriculum?"

"No," replied George. "But it was clear to me that those Catholics didn't let you fool around. I could see that on the first day I arrived."

"How so?" asked his father.

"When I walked to math class, I couldn't help but notice the guy they'd nailed to the plus sign."

PICK UP LINES

If I said you had a beautiful body, would you hold it against me?

Come and sit on my lap and we'll talk about the first thing that pops up.

FAILING IN STYLE

1. Once the examination paper has been distributed, run out of the room screaming "Paul, Paul, I've got the secret document."

2. See how many ethical reasons you can find to refuse to answer each question. Begin with your religious beliefs, but sexism, racism and dementia should not be forgotten.

3. Set fire to the examination paper.

4. Cry for your mommy.

5. Comment on how sexy the instructor looks.

6. Keep complaining the person next to you has stolen your answers.

7. Five minutes after the examination begins, start to laugh, walk to the front and give in a blank answer book. As you leave, say, "Boy, that's the easiest exam I'll ever ace."

8. Spend the time designing an examination paper for the instructor to answer.

9. Call the instructor over and demand he or she makes question one clearer. Insist it's badly written. Ask what they really want. After they have answered question one for you, call them back to answer question two.

10. Shout, "I attended every lecture! Where's the professor who taught this course? I can't understand a damn word of this! I'll sue!"

HEADLINERS

We are still awaiting the greatest headline of all time, "Pope Elopes." Nonetheless, here are a few golden oldies that you may have missed.

Reagan Wins on Budget, But More Lies Ahead.

Iraqi Head Seeks Arms.

Eye Drops Off Shelf.

Teacher Strikes Idle Kids, Again.

Tornado Rips Through Cemetery; Hundreds Dead.

Hollywood Finds Dwarfs in Short Supply.

Man Loses Ear, Waives Hearing.

Steals Watch, Faces Time.

Hospital Sued by 8 Foot Doctors.

Prosecutor Releases Probe into Accountant.

MEDICAL EMERGENCIES

"Nurse, how is the little boy who swallowed all those quarters?"

"Not much change yet doctor, I'm afraid."

• • •

"Well, Mrs. Adams, I've got some good news for you. The operation has been a big success. The incision is healing well and you can go home today. Be careful with housework; no cooking or heavy lifting."

"What about intercourse, doctor?"

"I'd love to Mrs. Adams, but I've another operation scheduled in twenty minutes."

• • •

The beautiful young woman sat down and opened her mouth wide. The dentist began to peer and probe.

I'm sorry," he said, "I'm going to have to drill those two molars."

"No, no," she cried. "I'd rather have another baby."

"Okay," said the dentist, "but let me re-adjust the chair, first."

SEXUAL PREFERENCE

An interesting study reports that if a "waitress" puts a smiley face near her name on a restaurant bill, her tip goes up an average of 19%. However, if a "waiter" does the same thing, his tip goes down an average of 3%! I think the lesson speaks for itself.

RETRACTION: COULD BE DIFFICULT

The 'Greek Special' is a huge 18 inch pizza and not a huge 18 inch penis, as unfortunately described in our advertisement of May 27th. Big Dick's Pizza would like to apologize for any confusion Tuesday's ad may have caused.

correction printed in a local newspaper

TRY THIS ON FOR SIZE

The midget, Eugene Bernays, was well known as a psychic. Years after his reputation in this field had been established, it was discovered that he also was a serial killer. Imprisoned and sentenced to death, he somehow escaped from police custody. An APB (All points bulletin) was issued seeking public assistance in his recapture. It began, "small medium at large".

BUSINESS ACUMEN

Everything that can be invented has already been invented.

> *Charles H. Duell,*
> *director of the U.S. Patent Office, 1899*

There is no likelihood man can ever tap the power of the atom.

> *Robert Millikan, Nobel Prize in Physics, 1923*

Heavier-than-air flying machines are impossible.

> *Lord Kelvin, president,*
> *Royal Society, 1895*

The information superhighway is a dirt road that won't be paved over until 2025.

> *Sumner Redstone, CEO*
> *of Viacom/Blockbuster*

This telephone has too many shortcomings to be seriously considered as a means of communication. The device is inherently of no value to us.

> *An internal Western Union*
> *memo, 1876*

I think there is a world market for maybe five computers.

> *Thomas Watson,*
> *IBM chairman, 1943*

MORE SHAMELESS ADVERTISING

Madame Speaker, a good catchword can obscure the truth for a generation. The history of our species is one of phrases, which suddenly rise to great power and then, just as quickly die away: the "merchants of death," "collective security," "the red menace," "peace in our time," "a chicken in every pot," "inspirational channellers," "alien abductions," "mind-melding insight," "android power," "reach for the stars," "animal rights," "alien business partners," and so on, and so on. At the time of their currency, very few individuals have either the courage or the resources to stand up against their tremendous force. They develop an irresistible authority, sweeping all before them like a tidal wave.

> *Harold D. Foster,* The Ozymandias Principles,
> *Southdowne Press!*

MISS DIAGNOSIS

A beautiful young woman paid a visit to her physician.

"Doctor," she said, "I'm so tired all the time that I can hardly get out of bed in the morning."

"Well," replied the doctor, "maybe you're doing too much housework?"

"No, it can't be that. I've got a maid, cook, and gardener. I hardly lift a finger around the house."

"What about exercise? Are you overdoing the aerobics, jogging, or tennis?"

"No, doctor," she answered, "I don't like to exercise. I swim a little once in a while, but only for a few minutes. I never visit the gym."

"Well, then," continued the physician, "How's your diet? Do you eat properly?"

"You needn't worry about that. I only eat organic foods and I take a vitamin and mineral supplement every day. I don't smoke or drink," she answered.

"How's your sex life? Are you getting enough sex?" enquired the doctor.

"I think so. I make mad, passionate love every night, but Sunday," she answered.

"Well, that's probably a bit excessive. Why not try cutting out Thursday night's activity? Let's see if that makes you any less tired," suggested the physician.

"But doctor, I can't do that," she cried. "My husband travels a lot in his job. That's the only night he's in town."

NOW CHEW ON THIS

Do you want the assistance of an expert in everything? Get married.
after Hal Magner

When I was fifteen, my father was so stupid, I could hardly bear to listen to him talk. By the time I was twenty-five, I was amazed to find how much he'd learned in only ten years.
Anon

THINK ABOUT THIS

People are like stained glass windows. They shine and sparkle when the sun's out, but when darkness sets in, their true beauty is revealed only if there is an inner light.

after Elizabeth Kubler-Ross

DR. EINSTEIN, I PRESUME?

This apparently true story is attributed to Churchill Einsenhart, son of the former Dean of Princeton's Graduate School. Shortly after Einstein's arrival on campus, the Dean's secretary received a telephone call.

"Can I talk to Dr. Eisenhart, please?" asked the caller.

"I'm afraid he's out," was the response.

"In that case," continued the speaker, "Can you tell me where Dr. Einstein lives?"

The secretary had been briefed that Dr. Einstein's privacy had to be protected at all costs and refused politely. The voice on the telephone dropped to a whisper, "Please tell me, I am Dr. Einstein and I've forgotten where I live."

after Einstein: The Life and Times *by*
Ronald W. Clark

The most beautiful emotion we can experience is the mysterious. It is the source of all true art and science. He to whom this emotion is a stranger, who can no longer wonder and stand rapt in awe, is as good as dead: his eyes are closed . . . To know that what is impenetrable to us really exists, manifesting itself as the highest wisdom and the most radiant beauty which our dull faculties can comprehend only in their most primitive forms—this knowledge, this feeling, is at the center of true religiousness. In this sense, and in this sense only, I belong to the rank of devoutly religious men.

Albert Einstein

WOULD I LIE TO YOU?

A bus full of politicians is speeding down a country road, tries to take a corner too fast and hits a tree. Hearing the noise, an old farmer goes over to see what has happened. He then returns to his farm for a back-hoe and proceeds to dig a large hole and bury everybody on board.

When the politicians don't turn up for their meeting, the local police chief comes looking for them, finds the damaged bus, and asks the farmer where the politicians went.

The old farmer describes the accident and explains that, to save the county any expense, he buried them all.

"But," says the police chief, "are you sure they were all dead?"

To this question, the old farmer replies, "Well, some said that they weren't, but ya know how them politicians like to lie."

YOUR SLIP IS SHOWING

On Thursday afternoon, there will be services in the north and south of the church. Infants will be baptized at both ends.

This being Easter Sunday, during the service, Mrs. Dennison will come forward and lay an egg on the altar cloth.

The Little Mothers' Club is enlarging its membership. Any women wishing to become a Little Mother should visit the minister privately in his study.

There will be a meeting of the Ladies' Liturgy Society on Friday night. One of the highlights will be Mrs. Grayson singing: "Put Me in My Little Bed," accompanied by the pastor.

The ladies of the church have cast-off clothing. If you are interested, they can be seen in the church basement, after the Wednesday prayer meeting.

On Sunday, the service will end with "Little Drops of Water." Mrs. Harper will begin very quietly and then the rest of the congregation will be asked to join in.

A Bean Supper will be held on Friday evening in the basement. It is expected that music will follow.

PROGRESS IN MEDICINE

A man was having terrible stomach pains and went to see his doctor. The physician prescribed three glasses of orange juice to be drunk during every meal. But, by the next day, the pain had become even worse, so the patient staggered back to the doctor's office. After listening to the man describe his stomach pains, the physician said, "Avoid orange juice at all costs."

"But doctor, only yesterday you recommended that I drink three glasses of orange juice with each meal," said the patient.

"Well, that just proves how fast we make strides in medical research," was the reply.

IT'S THE LAW

It is legal because I wish it.
Louis XIV

A law is not a law without coercion behind it.
James A. Garfield

The safety of the people shall be the highest law.
Cicero

Where law ends, tyranny begins.
William Pitt (senior)

What a cage is to the wild beast, law is to the selfish man.
Herbert Spencer

Laws . . . . are the product of selfishness, deception, and party prejudice. True justice is not in them, and cannot be in them.
Leo N. Tolstoy

There is plenty of law at the end of the nightstick.
Grover A. Whalen

NASTY LAWYER JOKE

A receptionist for a law firm was answering the telephone, soon after its senior partner had died, unexpectedly.

"Is Mr. Alan Jackson there?" asked the caller.

"No I'm afraid not," answered the receptionist. "I'm sorry to have to tell you that Mr. Jackson has just passed away."

"Is Mr. Alan Jackson there?" asked the caller.

"I'm terribly sorry, no he's not. He passed away last night," answered the receptionist.

"Can I speak to Mr. Alan Jackson?" the caller enquired again.

The receptionist was becoming perplexed and agitated. "Perhaps I'm not making myself clear to you sir, but Mr. Jackson is dead. He died last night."

"Is Mr. Alan Jackson there?" asked the caller yet again.

"Now just a minute. Are you deaf?" shouted the receptionist. "Can't you understand what I'm telling you? Mr. Jackson is DEAD."

"Oh, yes, I fully understand that," replied the caller, "I just can't hear it often enough."

SAD TO SAY

A 25-year old woman married an 89-year old man. They were deeply in love. Him with her and she with his money. A few months later, the young woman went to her doctor, because she was feeling a little under the weather. To her amazement, the physician told her she was pregnant. In a rage, she rushed to the nearest telephone and rang her husband.

"You old goat, you son of a bitch. You've got me pregnant," she shouted.

There was silence at the other end of the line. Eventually, her husband answered, "Who is that please? Who's calling?"

THE BOTTOM LINE

This is another story that was presented as true.

A lady decided to e-mail Valentine greetings to her son and his new bride. She wrote: HAPPY VALENTINE'S DAY TO BOTH OF YOU! LOVE MOM (She had to shout, she was a long way from Virginia). The message was sent to her new daughter-in-law's computer but was only partially transmitted. The next day, her son called, asking why she had felt the need to send his wife a message which read, "F YOU! LOVE MOM."

AFFAIR OF THE HEART

A married man is having a very torrid affair with his secretary. One lunch hour, they rush over to her apartment and spend the whole afternoon making passionate love. Then they fall asleep until 8 o'clock. Seeing the time, they get up quickly. The boss then asks his secretary to go outside and rub his white shoes on the lawn. This mystifies her but there is no time for an explanation, so she does as asked.

He rapidly drives home and is met at the door by his wife, who demands to know where he's been. He quickly replies, "My secretary and I spent all afternoon at her place, making mad, passionate love and then we were so tired we fell asleep. That's why I'm so late. I cannot tell a lie."

The wife looks at him, notices the grass stains on his white shoes and replies, "Don't give me that crap. You've been playing golf again with your buddies, haven't you?"

MORE TRUE LOVE

I haven't said a word to my wife in two years—I don't like to interrupt her.

I married Mr. Right. I didn't know it at the time, but his first name is Always.

OLD SMARTS

Had I died at Moscow I should have left behind me a reputation as a conqueror without a parallel in history. A ball ought to have put an end to me there.

> *Napoleon*

Generosity gives help rather than advice.

> *Luc De Clapiers Vauvenargues*

Abstinence from doing is often as generous as doing, but not so apparent.

> *Michel de Montaigne*

A boy can learn a lot from a dog: obedience, loyalty and the importance of turning around three times before lying down.

> *Robert Benchley*

Whenever I hear people discussing birth control, I always remember that I was the fifth.

> *Clarence Darrow*

The art of war is, in the last result, the art of keeping one's freedom of action . . .

> *Xenophon*

SHOER THING

As Gandhi stepped aboard a train, one of his shoes fell off onto the track. The train started to move and he had no time to retrieve it. To the amazement of his companion, Gandhi took off the other shoe and threw it back down the track, so it landed near the first. When asked why, he smiled and said, "Now the poor man who finds the first shoe lying on the track will have a pair to wear."

> *Anon*

INTELLIGENCE QUOTA

The peak years of intelligence lie between four and nineteen. At four, you know all the questions and by the time you reach nineteen, you know all the answers.

BLESSINGS

Blessed are they who can laugh at themselves, since they will have endless amusement.

LUCKY

A police officer had what he thought was a perfect hiding spot to detect speeders, but to his amazement, he wasn't catching anybody. After a few hours, he gave up and was driving down the road, when he noticed a small boy with a huge hand lettered sign which read, "RADAR TRAP JUST AHEAD." He turned the police car around and drove in the opposite direction where he saw the boy's accomplice, another kid, standing about 100 yards beyond the radar trap, with a sign that read "TIPS", and a bucket full of change.

NOT SO LUCKY

A motorist was caught in an automated trap by a system that used radar to measure his speed and a camera to photograph his licence plate. Later, he received a ticket in the mail for $100, together with a photograph of his automobile. Instead of paying the fine, he sent a photograph of a $100 bill to the police department. A few days later, he received a second letter from the police containing a picture of a set of handcuffs. He paid up.

EVEN LESS LUCKY

A man drinks too much at a party and refuses to listen to his friends when they try to stop him from driving. About six blocks from home, the police pull him over for weaving across the road and ask him to get out of his car and walk in a straight line. Just as he begins to attempt this, the police radio announces that a robbery is in progress in a house less than a block away. The police tell the suspected drunk to stay just where he is and they run off to the site of the robbery. As soon as they have gone, he climbs into his car and drives home. When he arrives there, he says to his wife that he's going to bed and that she should tell anybody who asks for him that he has been in bed all day with the flu.

An hour or so later, the police arrive, carrying his driver's licence, and ask to speak to him. His wife follows the plan and tells them he's too ill and has been in bed all day. The police then insist on seeing his car, so she takes them to the garage, where they find the police car, with its lights all still flashing.

FOOD FOR THOUGHT

A trickster pays a lady-of-the-night to visit a resthome. She enters the bedroom of an old man and announces, "I'm here to give you super sex."

To which he replies, "I'll take the soup. What type is it?"

FOOD FOR MORE THOUGHT

I never worry about diets. The only carrots that interest me are the number you get in a diamond.

Mae West

My children usually refused to eat anything that hadn't danced on TV.

after Erma Bombeck

There are three good reasons for breast-feeding: the milk is always at the correct temperature; it comes in attractive containers; and the cat can't get into it.

after Irena Chalmers

If this is coffee, please bring me some tea. If this is tea, please bring me some coffee.

Abraham Lincoln

YOU MAY SEE A STRANGER

In a monastery in Ohio, every day before breakfast, the Superior would chant, "Good Morning, Good Morning."

The Brothers would all be expecting to chant back, "Good Morning, Good Morning."

Most of them didn't mind this ritual, but one hated it and finally decided to rebel. On that particular day, after the Superior had chanted, "Good Morning, Good Morning," he replied, "Good Evening, Good Evening."

The Superior had excellent hearing and noticed one of his Brothers had broken with tradition. He immediately stood up again and chanted in response, "Someone chanted evening!"

DID I TELL YOU THIS BEFORE?

Some cause happiness wherever they go, others whenever they go.
Oscar Wilde

I desire no future that will break the ties of the past.
George Eliot

The most wasted of all days is the one without laughter.
e.e. cummings

The world is a comedy to those who think, a tragedy to those who feel.
Horace Walpole

Comedy is the clash of character. Eliminate character from comedy and you get farce.
William Butler Yeats

I could be content that we might procreate, without conjunction,
or that there were any way to perpetuate the world without this trivial
and vulgar way of coition; it is the most foolish act a wise man commits in
all his life.
Sir Thomas Browne

To let friendship die away by negligence and silence, is certainly not wise.
It is voluntarily to throw away one of the greatest comforts of this weary
pilgrimage.
Samuel Johnson

Man is a machine—man the impersonal engine. Whatsoever a man is, is due to
his make, and to the influences brought to bear upon it by his heredities, his
habitat, his associations. He is moved, directed, COMMANDED, by exterior
influences—solely. He originates nothing, not even thought.
Mark Twain

Her date was pleasant enough, but she knew that if her life was a movie, this guy
would be buried in the credits as something like 'second tall man'.
Anon

It is when one is on the lowest wheel of fortune, that the wheel turns round and
raises us. This evening your destiny begins to change.
Alexandre Dumas

It is amazing how complete is the illusion that beauty is goodness.

F. Dostoevsky

To know all is not to forgive all. It is to despise everybody.

Quentin Crisp

Of Man's first disobedience, and the fruit
Of that forbidden tree whose mortal taste
Brought death into the world, and all the woe.

Paradise Lost. Book i. Line 1.

ALIENS?

Don't forget, absence of evidence does not mean
evidence of absence.

after Carl Sagan

THEN AGAIN

Extraordinary claims always demand extraordinary proof.

after Carl Sagan

If triangles had a god, He'd have three sides.

Yiddish proverb

WORTH REPEATING

Our real blessings often appear to us in the shapes of pains, losses and
disappointments; but let us have patience, and we soon shall see them in their
proper figures.

Joseph Addison

There are two ways of spreading light: to be the candle or the mirror that reflects it.

Edith Wharton

The art of progress is to preserve order amid change and to preserve change
amid order.

Alfred North Whitehead

Worry is interest paid on trouble before it becomes due.

William R. Inge

ADVICE

Be very careful of the words you use. Keep them soft and sweet,
you never know from hour to hour which ones you'll have to eat.

Anon

FEAR AND GROWTH

You gain strength, experience, and confidence by every experience where you
really stop to look fear in the face . . . you must do the things you cannot do.

Eleanor Roosevelt

Man is the only animal that blushes. Or needs to.

Mark Twain

Confusion, indecision, fear: these are my weapons.

Adolf Hitler

Will Rogers can't have ever met a lawyer. Unfortunately, I have.

after Tim Yatcak

IN THE DRIVER'S SEAT

This one is probably just a figment of somebody's imagination, but it's funny.

Albert Einstein was on the lecture circuit, travelling from university to university
in a chauffeur-driven automobile. At each stop, he gave the same speech about
his theory of relativity.

One day, while they were driving to the next institution, the chauffeur remarked,
"Dr. Einstein, I've listened to you deliver the same lecture 35 times, I know it
word-for-word and I bet I could give it myself."

"I believe you," said Einstein, "but let's see if it's really true. Nobody knows
what I look like at the next university, so when we get there, just give me the
chauffeur's cap and you can introduce yourself as Einstein."

Things went exactly as planned as the chauffeur flawlessly delivered Einstein's
usual lecture. When it was over, he started to leave the podium but a hand shot
up. One of the professors in the audience then began to ask a very complex
question, filled with references to equations, formulae, and calculations.

The chauffeur was shaken for a moment and then said, "I am very surprised you
feel the need to ask such a simple question. Why, even my chauffeur knows the
answer to that! To prove it, I'll invite him up here to answer it for you."

WORTH THINKING ABOUT

One doesn't discover new lands without consenting to
lose sight of the shore.

Andres Gide

Ships are safe in the harbour, but that's not what
ships are for.

Unknown (but one of my fav's)

Let us cross over the river, and rest under the shade of the trees.

*Thomas J. "Stonewall" Jackson's last words before
dying on May 10, 1863 following the battle of
Chancellorsville in the U.S. Civil War*

There is a land of the living and a land of the dead and the bridge is love . . . .

Thornton Wilder

BATS IN THE BELFRY

Three ministers were discussing problems that they had in common. The first
said, "I've been having terrible bat trouble in my church. I've tried everything:
bells, sprays, cats, but nothing seems to work."

The second replied, "I know exactly what you mean. I've got hundreds living in
my belfry. I've even paid $2500 to fumigate the place, but those bats just won't
move out."

The third said, "I had bat trouble until I baptized them all and told them that
they'd have to donate 10 percent. Haven't seen one since!!"

REAL INSIGHTS

Children will not remember the material things that you provided but will always
recall the feeling that you cherished them.

after Richard L. Evans

Love is a fruit in season at all times, and within reach of every hand.

Mother Teresa

Keep away from people who try to belittle your ambitions. Small people always
do that, but the really great make you feel that you too, can become great.

Mark Twain

WHERE THERE'S A WILL

The patient shook his physician's hand and said, "Since we are such good friends, I don't want to insult you by offering to pay for all you've done for me. But, I just want you to be aware that you are mentioned in my will."

"I'm delighted to hear that," replied the doctor. "Would you mind giving me back the prescription for a moment, I just want to make one or two changes."

IN MY OPINION

My wife and I have opinions about every issue. When we discuss them, she gives me her opinions, then she gives me mine.

My church welcomes any and all denominations, but it actually prefers twenties and fifties.

The first time I visited the trophy shop, I looked at the stock and said to myself, "Gee, this guy must be good, real good."

APPLIED MATHEMATICS

Work this out as you read. Don't cheat by reading the ending first.
(You may need a calculator if you're not a math whiz.)

CALCULATION:

1. To begin, decide the number of days a week that you would like to have sex.

2. Multiply this number by 2.

3. Add 5.

4. Multiply the result by 50.

5. If you have had this year's birthday, add 1747. If not, add 1746.

6. Finally, subtract the four digit year that you were born.

RESULTS:

You should now have a three digit number. The first digit of this is your original number (that is, how many times you want to have sex each week.) The second two digits are your age!!! This should really work out. If it didn't, try again! This is the only year (1997) that it will work!

ARTIST AT WORK

When you are young, you see life as an enormous canvas and you paint with broad, carefree strokes. Then as you age, you realize that the canvas isn't really that big. Your brush strokes become increasingly deliberate and refined knowing that the painting will soon be finished and the artist will paint no more.

Anon

SIGNS OF THE TIMES

In my local video store, there is a large sign supported by a stand with feet that stick out dangerously in every direction. It reads, "Do not trip over sign."

Carved in stone, over the huge front doors of an old church, is the inscription "The Gates of Heaven." Below it is a cardboard sign which reads, "Use other entrance."

PARENT'S DICTIONARY

DUMBWAITER: asks if the kids would care for a second dessert.

FEEDBACK: baby doesn't like the strained carrots.

FULL NAME: what your child is called when he's been bad.

GRANDPARENTS: people who think your children are wonderful, despite the fact they're not being raised correctly.

HEARSAY: what toddlers always do after someone uses a dirty word.

INDEPENDENT: how we want our children to be, so long as they do what they're told.

PUDDLE: a little body of water that attracts other little bodies wearing dry clothes and shoes.

SHOW OFF: a child with more talents than yours.

STERILIZE: what you do to your first baby's pacifier by boiling it and to your last baby's pacifier by blowing on it.

TWO-MINUTE WARNING: when the baby's face turns red and she starts to grunt again.

WHODUNIT: none of your kids.

TEXAN BULL

Dallas salutes those who can buy art, not those who create it.
> *after A.C. Greene*

And now, will y'all stand and be recognized?
> *Texas House Speaker Gib Lewis to a group of*
> *handicapped in wheelchairs*

Ain't nothing in the middle of the road but dead armadillos and yellow stripes.
> *after Texas Agriculture Commissioner, Jim Hightower*

No thanks, once was enough.
> *Texas Governor Bill Clements, when asked if he had*
> *been born again*

If ignorance ever goes to $40 a barrel, I want drillin' rights on that man's head.
> *Texas Agriculture Commissioner, Jim Hightower*
> *expressing his support for former*
> *President George Bush's policies*

If it's dangerous to talk to yourself, it's probably even dicier to listen.
> *Jim Hightower, again!*

. . . idiots, imbeciles, aliens, the insane, and women.
> *From a law which was in force until 1918 in Texas.*
> *It regulated who could not vote*

This 'ere is a really competitive business.
> *A gas station owner explaining why he had greatly*
> *increased the price of his gasoline during the Kuwait*
> *invasion*

Let's do this in one foul sweep.
> *Texas House Speaker Wayne Clayton*

I want to thank each and every one of you for having extinguished yourselves
this session.
> *Texas House Speaker Gib Lewis*

There's a lot of uncertainty that's not clear in my mind.
> *Gib Lewis, again!*

There are still places where people think that the function of the media is to
provide information.
> *Don Rottenberg*

YOU CAN BET ON THIS

Horses, always horses . . . You were a lord if you had a horse. Far back,
far back in our dark soul the horse prances. He is a dominant symbol: he gives
us lordship . . . And as a symbol he roams the dark underworld meadows of the
soul . . . Within the last fifty years man has lost the horse. Now man is lost.
Man is lost to life and power—an underling and a wastrel.

D.H. Lawrence

GENETIC DOGGEREL

Cross a Cocker Spaniel
with a Rottweiler and
you get the perfect dog
for the philandering
ex-husband, a Cockrot.

Breed a Bull Terrier and a Shitzu
and its offspring is a Bullshitz,
gregarious, but tends to get
underfoot.

Cross a Pointer and a Setter to produce the perfect Christmas gift, the Pointsetter.

Breed an Irish Spaniel with an English Springer Spaniel to produce the Irish
Springer, a dog that is fresh and clean as a whistle, with a nice smell.

The Lab Coat Retriever, produced by crossing a Labrador Retriever and a curly
Coated Retriever, is a favorite choice of research scientists and technicians.

Cross the Newfoundlander and Basset Hound, if you want a Newfound Asset
Hound, a dog greatly sought after by financial advisors.

Watch out for that Terrier-Bulldog cross, the Terri-Bull.

Never expect the Bloodhound-Labrador cross, the Blabrador, to keep your secrets.

Ever seen the Malamute-Pointer cross, the Moot Point, its . . . oh, well no matter.

The Collie-Malamute cross, the Commute, is a dog for those who have to travel
to work.

The Deerhound-Terrier cross is a dog that's faithful to the very end, the Derriere.

COMPUTER SEX?

Computers must be female because:

6. As soon as you commit to one, you find a better, newer model.

5. Only their creator understands their internal logic.

4. All mistakes, no matter how small, are committed to memory for endless future reference and repetition.

3. The language they use to communicate with each other is incomprehensible to everyone else.

2. The message "Bad command or filename" is about as informative as "If you don't understand why I'm mad at you, then you can't expect me to tell you."

1   Once you're committed to one, you'll spend half your paycheck on accessories for it.

GET THAT JOB DONE, NOW

Happy the man, and happy he alone,
He, who can call today his own;
He who, secure within, can say,
Tomorrow do thy worst, for I have
lived today.
                                    Horace

MORE BUMPER SNICKERS

One day you're the dog, the next you're the hydrant.

After Q met Lorena Bobbit he became O.

Support wildlife: have a party.

People like you provide exercise for my middle finger.

A single fact shouldn't be allowed to ruin a good argument.

I'm cat furniture.

All stressed out and nobody to choke.

If you're handed a lemon reach for tequila and salt.

GET SMART IDEAS

Thanks to Steven for the following quotes:

Put all of your eggs in one basket and-watch that basket.

> *Mark Twain*

There are more fools among buyers than among sellers.

> *French proverb*

A status symbol is anything you can't afford but did.

> *Harold Coffin*

Part of the loot went for gambling, part for horses, and part for women. The rest I spent foolishly.

> *George Raft*

When prosperity comes, do not use all of it.

> *Confucius*

Drive thy business, let it not drive thee.

> *Benjamin Franklin*

Buy sound stock, wait till it goes up, and then sell it. If it doesn't go up, don't buy it.

> *Calvin Coolidge*

The day of decision is the day to act upon it.

> *Japanese Proverb*

Even the thousand mile road has a first step.

> *Japanese Proverb*

Love lives in a cottage or a castle.

> *Japanese Proverb*

A light purse is a heavy curse.

> *Benjamin Franklin*

Gentlemen, the market will fluctuate.

> *Bernard Baruch*

The greatest pleasure in life is doing what other people say you cannot do.

> *Walter Bagehot*

MORE SHAMELESS
LITTLE OLD LADY BASHING

A little old lady rings the local police station to complain
that her neighbor is indecently exposing himself. A squad
car is sent around to investigate, but the officers find that
the neighbor has painted the lower half of his window
black. As a result, all that can be seen from the little old
lady's kitchen window is a man with a bare chest.

"Madame," says one of the officers. "There's no law against
a man taking off his shirt. All you can see is his upper body."

"Yes," she replies, "but go upstairs to my bedroom and climb up
on my dressing table. Then tell me what you can see."

NAUGHTY JOKE

An elderly couple were driving to Georgia from Indiana. The wife was
particularly hard of hearing. In Tennessee, they were stopped by a state trooper
who asked to see the husband's licence.

The hard-of-hearing wife shouted to her husband, "WHAT WAS THAT HE
SAID?"

The husband shouted back, "HE NEEDS TO SEE MY DRIVER'S LICENCE."

The trooper asked where they were going.

The wife again enquired, "WHAT DID HE SAY?"

The husband replied, "HE WANTS TO KNOW WHERE WE ARE GOING?"

The trooper took the licence, looked at it, and said, "So you're from Indiana.
I went to Indiana once. In fact, I had the worst sex in my life there."

Again the wife shouted to her husband, "WHAT DID HE SAY?"

To which the husband replied, "HE THINKS HE KNOWS YOU!!!"

IN A WORD

The Bosnian government recently purchased 1500 septic tanks. As soon as the
army can get them to start, they're going to invade Serbia.

●●●

A dentist was acquitted recently on a rape charge. He had been accused of
filling the wrong cavity.

BROTHER, CAN YOU SPARE A DIME?

The Sunday New York Times estimated that by the time he reaches retirement age, Bill Gates will be worth an amount equal to the combined wages of every worker in the United States for one year—somewhere in the low trillions.

ANOTHER TRUE STORY

I have quite a boring life, so this story is one of the funnier ones. I was over at a friend's house and we were watching TV when his smoke alarm went off with a loud beeping noise. We both got up and were quite surprised as we had nothing cooking and neither of us smoked. He reached up with a broomstick and poked the smoke alarm several times when after many attempts the noise ceased. About 20 minutes later it happened again. This time he got up on a chair and touched the center button, at first finding no success, but after some diligent pressing the noise eventually ceased. This continued every 15 minutes and we determined that there was something quite wrong with the smoke alarm. In frustration, my friend removed the small 9-volt battery of the smoke alarm, but in 15 minutes, you guessed it, it went off again! We then determined that it must have a back up recharging system, which would seem to make sense when you consider what the product is meant for. This continued until late in the evening when I had to leave. I reached the front door and the beeping went off again, although we now realized that it was coming from my friend's pocket. It appears that his beeper had been going off all along and we had misinterpreted the sound.

FREEDOM

There is a road to freedom. Its milestones are Obedience, Endeavor, Honesty, Order, Cleanliness, Sobriety, Truthfulness, Sacrifice, and Love of Fatherland.

Adolf Hitler

DOCTOR, DOCTOR

"Doctor, you must help me. I have such a short fuse. I keep losing my temper and as a result, I'm being rude and violent with everybody."

"So what's the problem, then?"

"I just told you, you stupid son-of-a-bitch."

GET SMART IDEAS II

Lack of money is the root of all evil.

George Bernard Shaw

Money is the cause of good things to a good man, of evil things to a bad man.

Philo

The fates lead him who will—him who won't they drag.

Seneca

Many men go fishing all their lives without knowing that it is not the fish they are after.

Henry David Thoreau

The big profits go to the intelligent, careful, and patient investor, not to the reckless and over-eager speculator.

J. Paul Getty

Buy when everyone else is selling, and hold on until everyone else is buying.

J. Paul Getty

The secret of success is making your vocation your vacation.

Mark Twain

If you do what you've always done, you'll get what you've always got.

Anon (and false)

You never make big money in the market without getting in the way of danger.

Michael Steinhardt

The trick to getting rich is correctly sizing up supply and demand.

Jim Rogers

Value determines stock prices—eventually.

John Train

Trend is your friend.

Old Trader's Axiom

Old Money: New Money that has learned to survive.

John Train

When in doubt, duck.

Malcolm Forbes

Whenever I get caught between two evils, I take the one
I never tried.

Mae West

No individual raindrop ever considers itself responsible
for the flood.

Anon

A citizen can hardly distinguish between a tax and a
fine, except a fine is generally much lighter.

G.K. Chesterton

There are more important things in life than a little
money, and one of them is a lot of money.

Anon (and true)

No man can think clearly when his fists are clenched.

George Hean Nathan

The trouble with unemployment is that the minute
you wake up in the morning, you're on the job.

Lena Horne

If 50 million people say a foolish thing, it is still a foolish thing.

Anatole France

Personally, I'm always ready to learn, although I do not always like being taught.

Winston Churchill

There is no future in any job. The future lies in the man who holds the job.

Dr. George Crane

By working faithfully eight hours a day, you eventually get to be a boss and work
twelve hours a day.

Robert Frost

The truth is more important than the facts.

Frank Lloyd Wright

The greater the number of laws and enactments, the more thieves and robbers
there will be.

Lao-tzu

Power doesn't corrupt people, people corrupt power.

William Gaddis

DISAPPOINTMENT

"Miss Henderson," said the biology professor, "name the organ which if stimulated can expand to six times its normal size."

Miss Henderson gasped and, in a shocked tone, replied, "Dr. Simpson, that's an obscene question and the Dean will learn about it."

Unperturbed, the professor responded, "I have two things to say to you. Firstly, the answer is the pupil of the eye in dim light. Secondly, some day you are going to be very disappointed."

ELEMENTARY

Sherlock Holmes and Dr. Watson decide to go camping. They ride their horses across the moors for miles and then, on a calm, warm night, they pitch their tent and go to sleep.

At about 2:30 A.M., Holmes shakes Watson awake and asks, "Do you see the moon and the bright stars? How clear the night sky is. What do you deduce from that?"

Watson, half asleep, answers, "My dear Holmes, it's going to be excellent weather tomorrow. It'll probably be dry and sunny."

"No, Watson," Holmes answers, "somebody has stolen our tent."

MALE BASHING AGAIN

Q: What is the insensitive part at the base of the penis called?

A: The man.

Q: How do men resemble noodles?

A: They're always in hot water and lack any real taste.

Q: What is the difference between pigs and men?

A: Pigs don't turn into men when they drink too much.

MORE, TO THE POINT

Well timed silence hath more eloquence than speech.

Martin Tupper

The graveyards are full of indispensable men.

Charles de Gaulle

Until it has been accomplished, everything is theoretically impossible. A history of science in reverse could be written by assembling the solemn pronouncements of highest authority about what couldn't be done and what could never happen.

after Robert A. Heinlein

The best and most beautiful things in the world cannot be seen, nor touched . . . but are felt in the heart.

Helen Keller

GET SMART IDEAS THE THIRD

Don't forget until too late that the business of life is not business, but living.

B.C. Forbes

An idea is often a flaming vision of reality.

Joseph Conrad

Nothing great was ever achieved without enthusiasm.

Emerson

We are always getting ready to live, but never living.

Emerson

A hero is no braver than an ordinary man, but he is braver five minutes longer.

Ralph Waldo Emerson

Everything comes to him who hustles while he waits.

Thomas Edison

NOW BE HONEST,
DO YOU LIKE THIS BOOK?

Your manuscript is both good and original; but the part that is good is not original, and the part that is original is not good.

Samuel Johnson

SIGN HERE

Petition to ban the widespread misuse of dihydrogen monoxide. This chemical is known to result in excessive sweating and vomiting. It is the chief component of acid rain and can cause severe burns in its gaseous state. Inhalation can be fatal. It has been found to be present in cancerous tumors, the blood of patients with Alzheimer's and heart disease, and in the spinal fluid of those with multiple sclerosis.

Given all these known associations with diseases and with toxic substances, we the undersigned urge that dihydrogen monoxide use be banned.

_____

_____

A freshman at Eagle Rock Junior High won the first prize at the Greater Idaho Falls science fair with a petition like this one. He was attempting to illustrate that alarmists, using junk science, were spreading fear of everything in the environment. He asked 50 people to support the banning of dihydrogen monoxide. Forty-three said yes, six were undecided and only one knew that the chemical concerned was water. The title of his winning project was "How Gullible Are We?"

JUST DO IT NOW

Do not think of your faults, still less of others' faults; look for what is good and strong, and try to imitate it. Your faults will drop off, like dead leaves, when their time comes.

John Ruskin

There are only two ways to live your life. One is as though nothing is a miracle. The other is as though everything is a miracle.

Albert Einstein

It is not the critic who counts, not the man who points out how the strong man stumbles or where the doer of deeds could have done them better. The credit belongs to the man who is actually in the arena, whose face is marred by dust and sweat and blood, who strives valiantly, who errs and comes up short again and again because there is no effort without error and short-comings, who knows the great devotion, who spends himself in a worthy cause, who at the best knows in the end the high achievement of triumph and who at worst, if he fails while daring greatly, knows his place shall never be with those timid and cold souls who know neither victory nor defeat.

Teddy Roosevelt

FISHING FOR THE SECRETS OF LIFE

You can never have too much equipment.

If in doubt, exaggerate.

Everybody has a good story about the one that got away.

The best place to be is the top of the food chain.

Sometimes you've really got to squirm hard to get off the hook.

Cast everything in the best light.

Get reel!

Take off enough time to smell the fish.

A line has a hook at one end and an optimist at the other.

It is always better to fish at the other side of the lake.

Good things come to them who wade.

Still waters run deep.

Even your best lines loose their zip with overuse.

I BELIEVE

Found a society of Honest Men, and all the thieves will join it.

Alain

Women are never stronger than when they arm themselves with their weaknesses.

Madame Du Deffand

A man is as old as the woman he feels.

Groucho Marx

There was no respect for youth when I was young, and now that I am old, there is no respect for age. I missed it coming and going.

J. B. Priestley

Laughter is the language of the gods.

Buddhist saying

People are about as happy as they make up their minds to be.

Abe Lincoln

TWO MEDICAL EMERGENCIES

The psychiatrist received an emergency telephone message.

"My oldest daughter is hopping around in the backyard, picking up grubs and clucking like a chicken," said the caller.

"Good Lord," replied the physician. "How long has she been doing that?"

"Eight years," was the reply.

"But why didn't you call me sooner?" enquired the doctor.

"Well, it's like this. I have a large family and needed the eggs."

• • •

A doctor read the medical file of a new patient and discovered that the poor man suffered from severe migraine headaches for twenty years. He called the patient into his office and said, "Mr. Jones, I've just read your file and I see you've tried every other method possible to get rid of your headaches, including drugs, herbs, acupuncture, and vitamins and minerals. The sad truth is that you've already been given every treatment I learned in medical school, or have read about since."

"But doctor, I'm desperate. Isn't there anything you can suggest? These headaches are so bad lately, I've even been thinking of suicide," answered the patient.

"Well, to tell you the truth, there is one thing," replied the physician. "Once I suffered from migraine headaches myself but cured them in a novel way. You might try that."

"Anything. I'll try anything," said the patient.

"Well," continued the doctor, "when I feel a migraine coming on, I go home and take a very hot bath. I have my wife rub me all over with a soothing, scented herbal cream and then I make mad passionate love to her. Amazing though it may seem, this always works for me. Try it for six weeks and then come back to tell me if you notice any improvement."

The patient agreed to follow these instructions to the letter. Six weeks later, he returned, smiling and full of life.

"It worked, doctor! It worked! I feel wonderful."

"Excellent, excellent," replied the physician.

The patient continued to sit waiting.

"Is there something else?" enquired the physician.

"Well," replied the patient, "I'd just like to say I love the way you've decorated your bedroom."

THINK AGAIN

Although it is not true that all conservatives are stupid people . . . it is true that most stupid people are conservatives.

John Stuart Mill

Those who accept to reap the blessing of freedom, must, like men, undergo the fatigue of supporting it.

Thomas Paine

SPACE STATION

Soviet and US spokespersons regret the accident that put the residents of their space station at risk. After detailed investigation, it has been concluded that the accident was caused by one thing and one thing only:

OBJECTS IN MIR ARE CLOSER THAN THEY APPEAR.

AN AWKWARD SITUATION

I think this is a true story. It is supposed to have taken place at Denver's old Stapleton airport. If it didn't, it should have!

It had been foggy. Several flights had been cancelled and a single gate agent was rebooking a long line of inconvenienced air travelers. Suddenly, a very angry passenger pushed his way to the front, slapped his ticket on the counter and cried, "I HAVE to be on the next flight and it MUST BE FIRST CLASS."

The agent replied, "I'm sorry, sir. I'll be pleased to help you when it's your turn. I've got to accommodate the people in front of you in the line first. Once I've done that, I'm certain we'll be able to work out something."

The irate passenger was unimpressed. He asked very loudly, so the passengers in the line could hear, "DO YOU KNOW WHO I AM?"

Without a moment's hesitation, the gate agent picked up the microphone and over the public address system announced, "May I have your attention please, ladies and gentlemen. We have a passenger at the front of the line WHO DOES NOT KNOW WHO HE IS. If anyone can help identify him, please come to the gate."

Everybody in the line went into hysterics except the impatient passenger, who glared at the agent and, through gritted teeth, swore, "SCREW YOU."

Without blinking, she smiled and said, "I'm sorry, sir, but you'll have to join the end of the line for that too."

CAN YOU REPEAT THAT, AGAIN?

Three nuns were taking a long train journey and decided to make the time pass more quickly by confessing their worst sins. The first admitted, "Sex is my worst sin. I think about men constantly, dream about them at night, and can't live permanently without them."

The other two admit that this is a terrible sin.

"Wait," the first cries. "It gets worse. Once a year, I give up my habit for a week and become a lady of the night working constantly until I'm exhausted. Then I return to the convent and put everything I've earned into the poor box."

The other two nuns are shocked, but amazed at her honesty. The second then starts to confess her worst sin.

"Well," she says, "I'm addicted to strong drink. I always check the poor box early in the morning because I've discovered that once a year, somebody puts an enormous amount of money into it. I steal most of that and buy several crates of whiskey, that I hide in the tomb of a long dead nun. This supply keeps me going throughout the year."

The third nun is sitting very quietly and says nothing. The other two turn to her and demand, "It's your turn. We've both confessed our worst sins, now what's yours?"

The third looks at them and says, "I'm a terrible gossip. All my life I've never been able to keep a secret because I can't, for the life of me, keep my mouth shut."

BORING

After 25 years of marriage, a man goes to his doctor and complains that he and his wife were having trouble making love. In truth, he admitted, the whole process has become hum drum.

"Well," says the doctor, "you've got to change that. Go straight home, tear off all her clothes and make mad love on the living room floor."

The man thinks for a minute and then agrees. The next day, he comes back to see the doctor again. The physician asks him what happened.

"I went home. Grabbed her. Tore her clothes off, threw her to the floor and made passionate love," he replied.

"How was it?" asked the doctor.

"Well," replied the patient, "to be truthful it was the same old thing. I didn't get much of a kick out of it, but her bridge club certainly did."

HARE TODAY, GONE TOMORROW

A young man is driving down the highway when a rabbit starts to cross. The driver swerves, but hits the animal. Being a very sensitive individual, he stops his automobile and examines the rabbit which appears to be rather flat and very dead.

Just then, a young woman pulls over to the side of the road and joins him. She studies the rabbit for a moment and then returns to her car, extracts a can and sprays its contents onto the road kill. In moments, the rabbit is revived, jumps up and waves its paw at the two humans and then hops off across a field. After a few metres, it turns and waves again. It hops a little further and waves its paw yet again.

The man is totally astonished and asks to see the can. On it is a label which reads "Hare spray—restores life to dead hare. Adds permanent wave."

Okay, yes, I apologize for this one.

HE-MALE/E-MAIL: SIMILARITIES?

Those who have it would be devastated if it were cut off.

Those who have it think that those who don't are somewhat inferior.

Those without it, don't think it's worth all the fuss.

Some of those who lack it would like to try it themselves. This is known as e-male envy.

It's definitely more fun when it's up, but this reduces the amount of work that gets done.

In the distant past, its only purpose was to transmit the information that was needed to ensure the survival of the species. Today, most people use theirs for fun.

Be careful how you use it, or you'll catch a nasty virus.

If you overuse it, you'll find it harder to think coherently and to concentrate.

We tend to attach more importance to it than its actual size and influence warrants.

If you're careless about how you use it, it'll get you into a lot of trouble.

COGITATE ABOUT THIS

Anyone is to be pitied who has just sense enough to perceive his deficiencies.
Hazlitt

Our years, our debts and our enemies are always more numerous than we imagine.
Charles Nodier

Men shut their doors against a setting sun.
Shakespeare

I knew her before she was a virgin.
Oscar Levant

It's better to be quotable than to be honest.
Tom Stoppard

Make money and the whole nation will conspire to call you a gentleman.
George Bernard Shaw

WHAT'S IN A NAME?

The editor would like to take this opportunity to invite you to visit beautiful, British Columbia. He suggests the following itinerary for those who are unfamiliar with the province.

Begin at Mosquito Creek (near Kimberley), drive to Mosquito Flats (near Clearwater), fly to Mosquito Mountain (Queen Charlotte Island), then boat to Mosquito Lake (near Prince Rupert). From there, you can drive to Mosquito Crag and Mosquito Hills (both near Smithers). It is not far to Mosquito Pass (near Burns Lake). Retrace your steps for a side trip to Mosquito Bay (near Kitimat). Then take a boat trip to see the Mosquito Islets (Inside Passage) and Mosquito Harbor (near Powell River).

Anyone completing this scenic trip should apply to the B.C. Centre for Adventure Tourism for their free, "I Gave Blood in B.C." T-shirt and complimentary booklet, 'How to Deal with Very Aggressive Bears.' In a nutshell, this publication recommends hiking with friends who can't run as fast as you.

RELIGIOUS CONVERSION

I'm a born again atheist.
Gore Vidal

PRUNING THE FAMILY TREE

Robert Salmo, 36, was drunk and disorderly in a Winnipeg market. When told that the police were on their way, Salmo snatched a large hot dog, shoved it into his mouth, and ran off without paying for it. When the police arrived, they found him lying unconscious on the street. Paramedics later removed a six-inch wiener from his throat, but not before he had choked to death.

Allan Roberts, 27, had probably had a little too much to drink at a party in St. Louis, before he popped a blasting cap into his mouth, crushing it with his teeth. The resulting explosion blew off his lips and tongue and blew out all of his teeth. A friend had earlier wired the cap to a battery and put it into an aquarium in an effort to explode it underwater, but it had failed to go off. Trying to help, Roberts had grabbed the blasting cap and pushed it into his mouth crying, "This is how to set if off." He was right. Roberts survived, but only after extensive facial surgery.

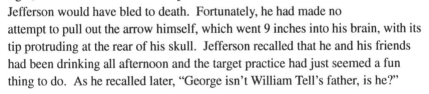

William Jefferson, 23, lost his left eye when a friend tried to shoot an empty beer can off his head. Doctors said that, if the arrow had been 1mm to the right, it would have severed a major blood vessel and Jefferson would have bled to death. Fortunately, he had made no attempt to pull out the arrow himself, which went 9 inches into his brain, with its tip protruding at the rear of his skull. Jefferson recalled that he and his friends had been drinking all afternoon and the target practice had just seemed a fun thing to do. As he recalled later, "George isn't William Tell's father, is he?"

Sidney Donaldson died on the slopes, while riding on a stolen foam pad. The accident occurred at 2 AM, after Donaldson and his friends had untied yellow foam protectors from some ski lift towers and carried them to the top of the run. These protectors were normally used to reduce injuries to skiers who accidentally hit the ski life support towers, but the group apparently used them as sleds to ride down the ski slopes. Donaldson, while travelling at great speed, hit one of the towers that no longer had its protector, dying instantly.

COULDN'T AGREE MORE

A short saying often contains much wisdom.

Sophocles

HAPPY DAYS ARE HERE AGAIN

Adolf Hitler was suffering from awful nightmares and decided to visit a psychic to find out the cause.

"I'm sorry," she said, "I'm not sure why you are having these terrible dreams, but I've discovered one thing of importance from my crystal ball."

"What's that?" enquired Hitler.

"Well, you will die on a Jewish holiday," she answered.

"And which of their holiday will that be?" he asked.

"I'm not sure," she said, "but I can tell you that whenever you die, it will be a Jewish holiday."

MAKING AN ASS OF HIMSELF

A priest decides that the best way to get the money he needs to renovate his church is to win a fortune gambling. Unfortunately, when he attends the auction to buy a race horse, he finds he only has enough money to get a donkey. Despite having serious doubts, he prays to the Lord for guidance and is told to purchase the animal and enter it at the nearby racetrack. This he does and the animal gets a great deal of attention when it comes in third. The headlines in the local newspaper read, 'PRIEST'S ASS SHOWS.' The cleric is so pleased with his share of the purse that he enters the donkey in another race, which it easily wins. The newspaper headlines read, 'PRIEST'S ASS WAY OUT IN FRONT.' Again, he is delighted with his winnings and enters the donkey in yet a third race. However, his bishop is so displeased with the unseemly publicity, that he orders the animal be withdrawn. The new headline then reads, 'BISHOP SCRATCHES PRIEST'S ASS.' This is rather too much for the bishop, who decides that the donkey must go. The priest, therefore, presents the animal to the mother superior at a nearby convent. This news is announced by the local newspaper with the headline, 'NUN HAS BEST ASS.' The bishop is now really upset and orders the mother superior to rid the church of the animal. This she does by selling it to a farmer for $20. The next day the headline reads, 'NUN PEDDLES ASS FOR TWENTY BUCKS.' The bishop has a heart attack.

BEST WISHES: NEW MOTHER

Congratulations. We all knew you had it in you.

Dorothy Parker

ONE STEP AT A TIME

A young priest is on his way to breakfast, when he meets two nuns.

"Good Morning, Sisters," he says.

To this they reply, "Boy did you get out of bed on the wrong side?"

This stuns the priest, because he thinks he has been very pleasant to them. A few moments later, he sees a Brother and greets him with the usual, "Good Morning."

To his surprise, his fellow priest answers, "Boy, did you get out of bed on the wrong side?"

This makes the priest quite angry, because he can't understand why everybody is picking on him. He continues on his way to the dining hall until he meets the Bishop.

Immediately, he says, "No, I didn't get out of bed on the wrong side and don't tell me that I did."

The Bishop looks amazed and says, "I wasn't about to mention beds, but I am curious about why you're wearing Sister Jane's shoes?"

THE ROOT OF ALL EVIL

I have discovered that all human evil comes from this, man's being unable to sit still in a room.

Blaise Pascal

He festooned the dung heap on which he had placed himself with sonnets as people grow honeysuckle around the outdoor privies.

Quentin Crisp on
Oscar Wilde

REST IN PEACE

Two women are talking. One confides that her late husband didn't have any insurance. The other notices her large diamond ring and asks how she'd managed to get it.

"Well," answers the first, "he was always concerned about his funeral. He saved $3,000 for his casket and $8,000 for a stone. This is the stone."

200 • *Gary Tooze*

SPANISH LESSONS

Two Mafia hitmen catch up with Jose in a downtown bar. One grabs him by the shoulders and says, "Jose, we want our damn money and we want it now. We know you stole it."

To which Jose responds, "No spicka de Engleesh."

The hitmen look around the bar and shout, "Anybody in here speak Spanish?"

Only the bartender replies, "I do."

"Tell him what we want," commands one Mafia hitman.

The bartender tells Jose in Spanish what they want. Jose keeps shaking his head and denies any knowledge of the missing money.

"Tell him we are SURE he took the cash and if he tells us where it is, we'll let him live. If we don't get it back right NOW, its curtains for him," says one of the hitmen.

Jose keeps shaking his head. Seeing this, the gangsters draw their guns. The bartender shouts at Jose, in Spanish, "For God's sake, they're going to kill you, if you don't tell them where it is."

Jose finally decides to spill the beans and, in Spanish, shouts, "The $500, 000 is under the third step from the top of the stairs at the front of St. Peter's church, fifth brick over from the right. I swear to God, I've not spent a cent."

"What was that he said?" asks one of the gangsters.

The bartender replies, "He says to tell you he knows nothing about any money and he ain't afraid to die."

SLICKER

A cowboy on a dude ranch is watching one of the guests trying to saddle a horse.

"Excuse me," he says politely, "but you're trying to put that saddle on backwards."

"Don't be so damn sure," the angry guest replies. "You don't even know which direction I'm going."

TOO TRUE

If we all pulled in one direction, the world would keel over.

Yiddish proverb

Falling in love is awfully simple. Falling out of love is simply awful.

You can only be young once, but you can be immature forever.

Anon

WORTH A MOMENT'S THOUGHT

Good resolutions are useless attempts to interfere with scientific laws.

Oscar Wilde

Who are the next knaves? Those who converse with them.

Pope

Explaining is generally half confessing.

Marquiss of Halifax

People do not lack strength, they lack will.

Victor Hugo

Happiness is not something you experience, it's something you remember.

Oscar Levant

Few people can be happy unless they hate some other person, nation, or creed.

Bertrand Russell

Women want mediocre men, and men are working hard to become as mediocre as possible.

Margaret Mead

A nice man is a man of nasty ideas.

Swift

It is not enough to possess wit. One must have enough of it to avoid having too much.

Andre Maurois

Whoever tells the truth is chased out by nine villages.

Turkish proverb

GREAT JOKE CONTEST

To finish off the volume, it was decided to hold a Joke Contest. All recipients of the *Quotations of the Day!* were invited to enter. The prize offered was a free copy of this book. What follows are the winning entries in no particular order. Congratulations to all.

AN UNORIGINAL REQUEST

Courtesy of F. Fergusson (by way of Matt Davis)

One spring afternoon, John was out in his garden weeding, when he noticed a hearse driving slowly past his house. Following the first hearse was a second. Behind this was a man dressed in black, a dog, and then some 250 men walking in single file. Intrigued by this strange funeral procession, John went up to the first man in the line and asked him who was in the leading hearse.

"That's my wife," was the reply.

"I'm terribly sorry," answered John. "What happened to her?"

"My dog bit her and she died."

John then asked the mourner, "Who is that in the second hearse?"

"That's my mother-in law. She died after she was bitten by my dog," came the reply.

John thought for a moment and enquired, "Would it be possible to borrow your dog for a few days?"

To which the new widower replied, "Join the end of the line."

DOCTOR SAYS

Sent in by Louis

A woman is standing admiring her breasts in the mirror when her husband comes home from work. He asks, "What are you doing?"

She replies, "Today, I went to the doctor for my checkup and he said that I had the breasts of a 25 year-old."

The husband is less than impressed and asks, "What did he say about your 55 year-old ass?"

To which she responds, "Frankly, my dear, your name never came up."

FLOWERY POSE

Originated by Fiona

Two little old ladies are sitting on a porch. One of them looks down the street and says, "Here comes my boyfriend, Fred, and he's carrying two dozen long-stemmed red roses. I know what that means. I'll be lying flat on my back all night with my legs in the air."

To which the other replies, "What's the matter dear? Don't you have a vase?"

EVERLASTING LOVE

Sent in by Cheryl

A man and his wife were sitting side-by-side on the sofa when, out of the blue, she asked him, "What would you do if I died suddenly?"

To which he replied, "I'd be heart-broken, devastated. But why are you asking me a question like that? You're not seriously ill, are you?"

"No, nothing like that," she said. "Would you remarry?" she persevered.

"No, of course I wouldn't," replied the husband.

"Don't you enjoy being married?" she asked.

"Well, yes darling. You know I do. Alright then, maybe I'd remarry."

"Would you sleep with your new bride in our bed?" asked the wife, after a long pause.

"Well, yes. Under the circumstances, I suppose I would," he answered.

"I see," said his wife. "And would you give her my jewelry and best clothes?"

"If there was anything she wanted to wear, I suppose I would," replied the husband.

"Really," said the wife very icily, "and would you take down the pictures of me and replace them with photographs of her?"

"Yes," said her husband. "Under the circumstances, I think that would be proper."

"Is that so," said his wife. "AND I SUPPOSE THAT YOU'D GIVE HER MY GOLF CLUBS TO PLAY WITH," she shouted.

"Don't be silly, dear," replied the husband. "Why would I do that? She's left-handed."

PUNISHING WEATHER FORECAST

Sent in by Greg

In the days of the former Soviet Union, a young married couple were out walking when something touched the tip of the husband's nose.

"I think it must be rainink," he said.

"No, no, my darlink, that's snow," his wife replied.

"Nyet, my little one, that was rain," he answered.

"You're wrong, my dear, wonderful, foolish husband," she responded.

They argued backwards and forwards about the weather and the temperature until they saw, on the other side of the street, Rudolph Doriniski, the Party Chief in Moscow.

"Look, there's the Party Chief," the husband shouted. "Let's ask HIM to decide if it's snow or rain."

They crossed the street and asked the Chief. He replied, "Rain" and walked on.

"You see," said the husband, "I was right."

"Nyet," replied the wife. "I'm still sure it was snow."

The husband sighed heavily and replied, "No No. You see . . . Rudolph (the Red) knows rain dear."

COMING OR GOING?

Sent in by Mae

Two nuns are cycling down a French country road. One turns to the other and says, "You know, I haven't come this way in years."

"Well Sister," says the other, "it's probably the cobblestones."

MEDICAL ASSISTANCE NEEDED

Sent in by Melanie

John goes to his physician, complaining that his body is wracked with pain.

"Now tell me exactly what's the problem," says his doctor.

"Well, it's like this. When I poke my chin, it's really painful. It hurts like mad if I poke my arm, or my ribs. It even hurts when I poke my knee," replies John.

The physician is very worried and immediately sends him for a full body X-ray. He is relieved by the consultant's report which reads, "Broken finger".

ROCKING THE BOAT

Submitted by Bill

An atheist decided to go on a fishing trip to Scotland. He hired a small row-boat and began to try his luck on Loch Ness. Suddenly, a fearsome monster rose out of the water, lifting his small boat high into the air. The fisherman looked down and could only see a gaping mouth filled with great white teeth, waiting for him to fall. Instantly, he cried, "Oh God, please save me from being eaten alive by this monster."

Immediately, a deep voice boomed from the Heavens above, "I thought you didn't believe in Me?"

"God, please, give me a break. Until about ten seconds ago, I didn't even believe in the Loch Ness monster," replied the fisherman.

RUSH JUSTICE

Sent in by Amie

Rush Limbaugh and his chauffeur were taking a drive in the country when a pig ran out onto the road. Unfortunately, they were going too fast to stop in time and so killed it. Limbaugh insisted that the decent thing to do was to drive to the nearby farm and confess that they'd killed one of the farmer's pigs. This they did, but Limbaugh sent his chauffeur inside to face the music. The man was gone for almost an hour. When he came back, Limbaugh asked why he had taken so long.

"Well," replied the chauffeur, "they gave me wine, fruit, cake, and insisted I sign my autograph."

"But what did you tell the farmer?" Limbaugh asked.

The chauffeur answered, "Just what you told me to say. That I was Rush Limbaugh's driver and I'd just killed the pig."

WAKE-UP CALL

Sent by Mae

Mrs. Westchester goes to have a private talk with her minister.

"Reverend," she said, "I'm embarrassed to say that my husband keeps falling asleep during the Sunday sermon. What can I do about it?"

The minister replies, "I have an idea. Take this hat pin. When I see your husband falling asleep, I'll signal and you can poke him in the leg with this pin."

Next Sunday, Mr. Westchester began to doze off. The vicar notices this and just after he's asked, "Who laid down his life for you?" he nods to Mrs. Westchester.

"Jesus!" cries her husband as his wife jabs him in the leg with the hat pin.

"Yes, Mr. Westchester, you are right," responds the minister and continues on with the sermon.

A few minutes later, Mr. Westchester begins to nod off again, just at the point where the vicar asks, "Who is your redeemer?"

The minister nods to the sleeper's wife who responds by jabbing her husband in the leg again.

"God!" cries Mr. Westchester.

"Right again," shouts the vicar as he resumes his sermon.

All too soon, Mr. Westchester starts to doze off again, but the minister doesn't notice. He continues his sermon and reaches the point at which he asks, ". . . and what did Eve say to Adam after she bore him 28 children?" At this point, Mrs. Westchester notices her husband is asleep and sticks him with the hat pin.

Suddenly, awakened, he shrieks, "Don't stick that damn thing into me again. I've had more than I can stand already. If you do, I'm going to break it off!!!"

SORRY MY MISTAKE

Sent in by Scott

The huge computer completely dwarfed the two mathematicians standing waiting for its output. A sliver of paper emerged from its vitals and one of the mathematicians studied it carefully for a few minutes. He then turned to his companion and said, "Do you realize it would take five hundred mathematicians three hundred years to make an error this big?"

HOME EDUCATION

Sent in by Cheryl

Little Billy comes home from school with a note from his teacher. It reads, "Billy seems to be having trouble telling the difference between little girls and boys. Please sit him down and explain what they are to him."

Billy's mother takes him by the hand, leads him upstairs to his bedroom and closes the door.

"Now Billy," she says. "I want you to remove my blouse."

So he unbuttons her blouse and takes it off.

"Billy, take off my skirt," his mother says.

Billy does as he is told.

"Now remove my bra." Billy does as ordered.

"Okay, Billy. Take off my panties."

The child again does as he is told.

"Now, my boy," his mother says, "don't you ever wear any of my clothes to school again!"

STANDING UP FOR HIMSELF

Sent in by Mae

A woman has been very unfortunate in love, but decides to take one more chance and puts an advertisement in the personals. It reads, "Beautiful, lonely woman looking for a man who will not hit me or run away and is incredible in bed."

A few nights later, her door bell rings and waiting outside is a man with no arms or legs, sitting in a wheelchair.

"I've come in answer to your advertisement," he says.

The woman replies, "I don't think so. You're not exactly what I had in mind."

"But," replies the man, "wait a minute, I have no arms and no legs . . . . so I can't hit you or run away."

The woman thinks for a minute and then asks, "So, how are you in the bedroom?"

To which he replies, "I rang the doorbell, didn't I?"

RINGING THE BELL AGAIN

Sent in by many recipients

Quasimodo's death leaves the Bishop of Notre Dame with a serious bell-ringer shortage. He decides, therefore, to have a competition to see who can best replace the hunchback. Several applicants demonstrate their bell ringing abilities and the bishop is just about to choose one as a replacement, when a man with no arms asks to be allowed to audition for the job. The bishop reluctantly agrees, despite the fact that he is baffled by the applicant who cannot hold the bell ropes.

The armless man, however, climbs up the tower stairs, runs towards the bell and bangs his face against its metal sides. The bell begins to ring. In next to no time, he is playing wonderful music. Amazed, the bishop is just about to hire him when the man, dazed by his efforts, trips and falls to his death. The bishop immediately rushes down the staircase to the street, only to find a large crowd gathering around the deceased applicant.

"Who was he?" demands someone in the crowd.

"I'm sorry. I don't know his name," replies the bishop, "but his face certainly rings a bell."

MORE HOME EDUCATION

Sent in by Sue

A young guy goes into a pharmacy to buy condoms. The pharmacist asks him whether he wants 3, 9, or 12 of them, since they come in small, medium, and giant packets.

"Well," the guy says, "tonight I'm going to have dinner with my hot new girl-friend's parents. Then we're going out to a dance and I think TONIGHT'S THE NIGHT. Once she finds out just how great I am, she'll have trouble keeping her hands off me, so give me the giant size!"

The young man makes his purchase and leaves. Later that evening, he sits down for dinner with his new girlfriend and her parents. He immediately asks if he can give the blessing. They agree, but are amazed to find he rambles on for several minutes, providing the longest grace they'd ever heard.

His girlfriend leans over and quietly says, "I'm amazed. You never told me that you were so religious."

He whispers back, "And you never told me your father was a pharmacist."

ANOTHER RUSH TO JUSTICE

Sent in by Melissa

A woman who has just won the lottery decides to buy the most expensive car money can buy. This is a state-of-the-art computer enhanced, dream machine. She drives it out of the show-room and down the highway. After a few minutes, she decides that music would be nice and searches for the radio. The dashboard looks like a jumbo jet's. After pushing and pressing a hundred different buttons, she drives back to the showroom in a rage. Once there, she screams at the salesman that there's not even a damn radio in the car. He assures her that she has the world's best automobile radio but that it's voice controlled and doesn't have buttons. To demonstrate, he calls out "Classical" and immediately Brahms begins to play. "Blues" he says and a B.B. King classic fills the air. Pacified, she drives off amazed.

Once back on the highway, she calls out "Country" and immediately a Garth Brooks tune comes on. A few moments later, she shouts "Folk" and Joan Baez begins to sing.

She's delighted with this new innovation and isn't paying much attention to her driving. Suddenly, another automobile runs a red light and almost hits her car.

"HALF-WIT," she screams.

The radio changes channels. "Good morning, everyone. This is the Rush Limbaugh show."

IN A MOMENT

Sent in by Leone

A young man was praying and to his amazement, he thinks he hears God answering his prayers. He thinks for a moment and asks, "God, how long is a million years to you?"

The Lord replies, "To me, my son, a million years is like a second of your time."

Then the young man asks God, "What is a million dollars like to you?"

To which the Lord replies, "To me, my son, a million dollars is just like one of your pennies."

This amazes the man who begins to feel courageous and asks, "God, could I have a couple of your pennies?"

God smiled and answered, "Why of course, in a minute."

DOING IT ON FAITH

Sent in by Inga

George and Alice were celebrating their 50th wedding anniversary. George decided to ask his wife whether she had ever been unfaithful to him.

She replied, "Three times."

George thought this over and decided that although three times in fifty years wasn't perfect, it could have been much worse. He then asked Alice, "When was the first time?"

"Do you remember when the bank manager refused you your start-up business loan, but then suddenly changed his mind?" she replied.

After a moment, George decided that really she'd only had his best interests at heart so he couldn't get too mad.

"When was the second time?" George enquired.

"Well, do you remember when your heart condition was so bad that no doctor would risk an operation, until Dr. Adamson suddenly changed his mind and saved your life?" Alice answered.

George realized that if it hadn't been for Alice's infidelity, he would not be alive, so he just kissed her.

"What was the third time?" he asked.

"Well, do you remember when you wanted to be lodge president, but figured you'd be 28 votes short and were really surprised when you won?"

GREATER PUNISHMENT

Submitted by Bernie

A painter was under contract to renovate a church. After he had finished two sides of the building, he realized that he hadn't bought enough paint. If he drove to the store for more, it would take considerable time and the cost would cut into his profits, so he decided to thin the remaining paint to make it stretch. When the job was completed, he was admiring his handiwork, when it started to rain heavily. Slowly, the thinned paint washed off and the old color could clearly be seen underneath. At that moment, the vicar looked out and saw what had happened. He then went outside and spoke to the painter, who confessed what he had done.

The vicar, wishing to ease the painter's burden, said, "Repaint my son, and thin no more."

GUMPY

Sent in by Dave

Florest Grump dies and arrives at Heaven's pearly gates. St. Peter explains that the place is filling up fast and he'll need to pass an exam to get in.

The first question St. Peter asks is, "How many days in the week begin with T and what are they?"

Grump thinks for a minute and answers, "Two, today and tomorrow."

St. Peter is a little taken-aback but replies, "Well, that's not the answer I was expecting, but it seems correct. So I'll ask you the second question. How many seconds are in a year?"

Grump thinks for a moment and replies, "Twelve, January 2nd, February 2nd, March 2nd, and so on to December."

St. Peter laughs, "Well that's not exactly the answer I was expecting, but we'll press on. The final question is, What is God's name?"

"Well," replies Grump, "that's an easy one. It's Howard."

"How in Heaven did you come up with that? asks St. Peter.

"You know," replies Grump. "Our Father, who art in Heaven, Howard be thy name."

MALE FLOWERS

Sent in by Harry

When a business was about to open, a close friend of the new owner decided to send her flowers. He arrived at the "Grand Opening," accepted a glass of white wine and a warm handshake from the host, and then wandered around looking at the floral arrangements well-wishers had sent.

He was amazed to see his own offering with a card attached which read, "Rest In Peace."

Angered by the error his florist had made, he rang up and vented his anger. After several minutes he stopped and waited impatiently for the florist's explanation.

"Sir, I'm very sorry about the mistake but think of this: not very far away a large funeral is in progress, and there is a beautiful floral tribute on the casket with a note which says, "Congratulations On Your New Location."

DOG GONE

Sent in by Rasheed

Two Irish nuns have just arrived in the United States by boat. Once ashore, they see a sign "hot dogs."

"Do you mean to say," asks one, "that the people here eat dogs?"

"Yes," replies the other, "I think that's true."

"Well," answers the first, "when in Rome, do as the Romans do. I'm hungry and I'm going to try one."

The other agrees that it's time to eat and they both order a hot dog from the vendor.

The nuns then take their hot dogs, wrapped in foil, to a bench nearby and begin to open them. The mother superior unwraps hers first, then staring cautiously, asks the other, "What part of the dog did you get?"

ON THE EDGE

Sent in by Cheryl

John and Martha lived in a small apartment in the city where their sex life suffered because of the presence of their nine-year-old son. One Sunday they decided they were desperate to make love and decided to send him onto the balcony and pay him to report on all the activities in the neighborhood. To a young boy, they thought, this type of spying would be entertaining and would distract him for the necessary hour.

The boy stood outside and called, "There's a car being towed away from the parking lot."

A few moments later, he shouted, "An ambulance just drove down the street."

Deciding he was suitably preoccupied, they began to make mad, passionate love. A minute later, however, their son called out, "The Johnsons have company arriving and the Smiths are having sex again."

At this, his parents shot bolt upright in bed. "How do you know that?" his amazed father asked.

"Well," their son replied, "their kid is out on the balcony."

NO MAN IS AN ISLAND

Sent in by Melissa

I believe Gilligan's Island was so popular because each of the seven characters in it represented one of the seven deadly sins. However, there is a flaw in this theory when you consider Gilligan, himself.

Consider, first, the Professor, who fits PRIDE to a T. Anybody who can make a ham radio out of two coconuts has to feel pretty sure of himself.

Mary Ann is obviously a prime example of ENVY. Despite all the skimpy tops, she could never quite achieve Ginger's glamour.

Who can doubt that Ginger is LUST incarnate? It is clear what being deprived, episode after episode, was doing to her. That glazed look, my friends, wasn't boredom.

Who would take a trunk full of money on a three-hour cruise? Mr. Howell is without a doubt a clear case of GREED.

That leaves us with three characters and three deadly sins. It's easy to see that Mrs. Howell, who did absolutely nothing during her years on the island, must represent SLOTH.

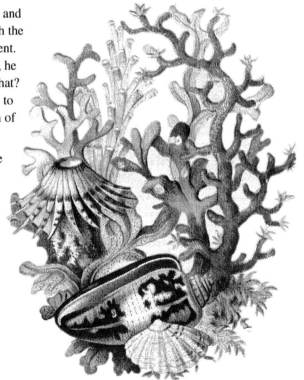

There remains only ANGER and GLUTTONY, either of which the Skipper could clearly represent. Remember how, when angry, he used to hit Gilligan with his hat? The Skipper, always anxious to eat, probably represents both of these sins.

On Gilligan's Island then, we have all of the Seven Deadly Sins, repeated endlessly in a recurring Hell of Hope, Denial and Despair, where all seven characters are trapped until the last TV re-run ends. Why are they there? Who is responsible?

Gilligan.

Gilligan is SATAN.

INTERVIEW TECHNIQUE

Sent in by Lisa

Three applicants are sitting in the waiting room for their turns to be interviewed for a high paying job.

The first is called in. The interviewer says to him, "Look at me and tell me something about myself that is unique."

The interviewee cries, "Well, that's easy, you haven't got any ears!"

The interviewer is clearly very angry and scribbles down a comment on a sheet and quickly calls for the second applicant.

When she enters, he says to her, "To test your observation skills, please take a close look at me and tell me anything you see that is unique."

The applicant is silent for a while and then says, "Well it appears that you've no ears."

Again the interviewer scribbles something down and then quickly calls for the third interviewee. As the second leaves the office, she mentions to the last applicant not to say a word about missing ears, since the interviewer is clearly very sensitive about it.

The interviewee sits down and is immediately asked, "Sir, would you please look at me and see if you can notice anything about me that is unique?"

The man thinks for a while, then says, "You're wearing high quality contact lenses."

The interviewer is delighted and cries, "Excellent! Excellent! You're just the type of astute individual this company is looking for."

The interview continues in a very positive way and the man is certain he's going to be offered the job.

At the end, the interviewer says, "By the way, one last question, how did you know I was wearing contact lenses?"

"Well," replied the applicant, "it was easy. You can't wear glasses. You've got no bloody ears."

BOX HIS EARS

Sent in by Druid

Question: What's the difference between a Metallica concert and a Holyfield-Tyson heavy-weight boxing match?

Answer: After a Metallica concert, you have a ring in the ears; after the bout, it's the other way around.

• • •

I stand by all the misstatements that I've made.

Gary W. Tooze aka Dan Quayle

This is not the end. It is not even the beginning of the end. But it is, perhaps, the end of the beginning.

Winston Churchill and Gary Tooze